SNOWDONIA CYCLE GUIDE

Snowdonia/Eryri Cycle Guide and Companion

CONWY TO MACHYNLLETH, CAERNARFON TO BALA

Phil Horsley

ISBN: 978-1-84524-230-5

Cover design: Lynwen Jones
Illustrations by Rosie Horsley

Published by Llygad Gwalch,
Ysgubor Plas, Llwyndyrys,
Pwllheli, Gwynedd, Wales, LL53 6NG

www.carreg-gwalch.com

Dedicated to Niamh, Maeghan and Samina

Remembering Richard Ballantine 1940-2013,
cycling evangelist

Snowdonia/Eryri

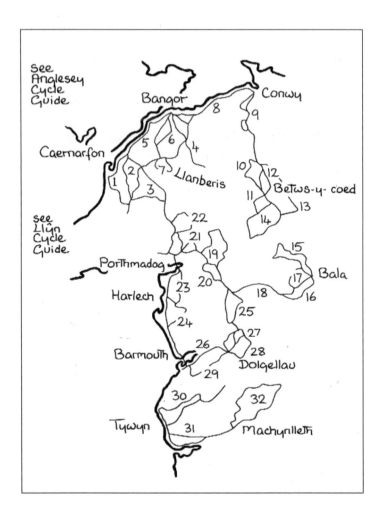

Contents

Betws-y-coed

Bala

Blaenau Ffestiniog

Porthmadog

Harlech and Dyffryn Ardudwy

Coed y Brenin

Dolgellau

Tywyn

Machynlleth

Introduction

Bookshelves groan with words in enthusiastic praise of the grandeur of Snowdonia, but in truth, in times past among visitors from England Snowdonia has had a reputation. The mountaineer F. S. Smythe, writing in 1940, describes the romantic English Lake District as 'vivacious' and 'sparkling', but for him Snowdonia is 'sombre, sad and lonely', and even 'gloomy'.

I've never been much for wearing my heart on my sleeve, but cycling the lanes and tracks of Snowdonia, from Conwy to Machynlleth, Bala to Caernarfon, many's the time I've stopped and stared in wonder and my spirits have been lifted. Cycling in Snowdonia is not easy, but it makes you feel alive and glad to be here on Earth.

Please note: this is NOT a mountain bike guide. Such guides are obtainable from bookshops, bikeshops and the mountain bike centres at Coed y Brenin and Llechwedd. Off road cycling in Snowdonia is subject to special access agreements. This book does contain runs through forests and on cycleways but they are on trails and cyclepaths and they do not need a specialist bicycle.

Disclaimer
I have done my best to verify the information in this book, but time passes, things change, I am a fallible being, and sometimes it is difficult to detect the difference between fact and fiction (if indeed there is a difference). All opinions expressed within are the responsibility of the author, and no-one else.

Cycling in Snowdonia, an overview

In the 1930's Ward Lock published the Red Guides:

'Cycling

Although the mountainous character of the country makes cycling in north and central Wales more arduous than in the south and east of England, it is by no means impossible to tour the country awheel. Generally speaking, there is less choice of route than in the regions of low relief, and while the main roads are apt to be crowded with fast-moving traffic, the by-roads frequently present stretches with steep gradients and indifferent surfaces.'

Do not be downhearted. While the above remains true today, with a little effort and a little knowledge cycling in Snowdonia is simply stunning.

Cyclists in Snowdonia come in bunches, like bananas. You can be riding along for a couple of hours with just yourself for company, then, hey presto, bore da's are flying and eyes are critically examining your geometry. Some of these fellow travellers are just ordinary folks, but others are specialists, devotees of either the off-road, adrenaline-rush descents (I've yet to meet a mountain biker who enjoys going uphill), or the growing band of road cyclists bent on achieving harmony with their machine to cover ground. The official routes attract cyclists, the trails (Lôn Eifion, Lôn Ardudwy, Llwybr Mawddach (Dolgellau these days hums with cyclists), Lôn Las Menai and Lôn Las Ogwen) and the Sustrans routes, Route 5 along the northern coast and Route 8 south from Bangor, are all popular. Other routes are signed, but have yet to reach the heights of popularity of the above, and there are plenty of other runs which are a joy to ride.

The Grading of Cycle Runs

I have had to throw out the grading system I used on the **Llŷn and**

Anglesey Cycle Guides, with the bathwater as it were. There are some fine family rides here, notably the cycle trails, and longer rides you can create for yourselves by coupling two or more rides together. Road cyclists tend to go for longer runs on the valley roads, with or without the mountain passes, but normally they don't tend to bother with the smaller roads which form the core of this book. Distance is not the only decisive factor when it comes to grading in Snowdonia. Of equal importance is the climbing involved. A friend can cover great distances, but he struggles on the hills, mainly because he's a smoker (he has an ashtray taped to his handlebars). It is, of course, true that the more you do the better you become.

So here is a somewhat subjective system. The more bikes there are, the harder the ride, from 🚲 to 🚲 🚲 🚲 🚲 🚲.

Let's Talk About Hills

Snowdonia doesn't do things by half. I recently cycled in Flemish Brabant, which has a 3 star grading for hills, all of which, in Snowdonia wouldn't even register. So I turned to the experts, *www.climbbybike.com*, and learned about supercompensation, aerobic and anaerobic thresholds, power-to-weight ratio, bmi etc. To put it simply hill climbing is controlled by 2 things; heart beat and cadence, your body and your bike, (see later for more details). The website has an enormously complicated formula to rank climbs, depending ultimately on length, height gained and average gradient. Not having a computor on board I would be guessing, so my index is based on a) whether or not I have to get off and push, and b) what the climb feels like. As a system it may not be perfect.

The Weather

It is misleading to characterize the weather in Snowdonia as mild and wet. The presence of such dominant mountain blocks produces huge climatic differences. In Summer the highest rainfall is where you would expect, on the highest mountains, Snowdon, the Glyderau, the Carneddau and Cadair Idris. Blaenau Ffestiniog is the second wettest town in Britain, after Fort William, with 79 inches p.a. (compared to 180 inches on the eastern flank of Snowdon). A few miles further north, Llandudno averages just 30 inches. The warmest places are Bangor, the Conwy valley, Porthmadog, Dolgellau and the Dyfi valley; the driest places are all around the coast, and the places with the most sunshine are Llandudno, Harlech and Barmouth.

Special mention should be given to the *föhn*, when moist air dries out and warms up as it descends from the mountains. Thus, Aber, on the northern coast, has registered temperatures of 18.3 degrees in January, and 21.3 degrees in November.

Cycling

Cyclists come in all shapes and sizes. On the one hand you have Scarlet, aged 6, on the other there was Jacques Anquetil ('You can hear him catching you. You don't have to look around. There is the hoarse sound of breath being drawn in gulps, and then he's past you. Then it's like being in a thunderstorm, with the sweat simply pouring off him as he goes by'. Tommy Simpson, except he was based in Yorkshire so you need to delete some 'h's and add a few 'bah gum's.)

Where I grew up everyone rode a bicycle, apart from the Brewer, the Headmaster and the Vicar, who took to a shire horse when drink took away his drivers license. My driving test was conducted in second gear because it coincided with the docks turning out for dinner.

The modern trend is for road bikes, the aspiration being a carbon-framed machine which will enable you to cover the hundred miles in five hours or so. Has the fashion for mountain bikes peaked? The range of bikes continues to grow: electric bikes are on the up, recumbents never really caught on, fixed-wheel are city bikes really, and a local chap is importing second hand bikes from Holland, big on comfort, big on wind resistance. My bike is old, a 5-3-1 tourer, but it is comfortable and it gets me around. Whatever suits you. There are no dos and donts. Lycra is not compulsory. Cycling is a World of Tolerance. Nonconformists, Anarchists, Lords and Ladies, hypochondriachs, Chavs and Neds, all are welcome. Cycling is good for you; for your heart, your immune system, your mental health, your strength. It wards off alzheimers, warts, arthritis, lunacy. It expands your view of the World, and, in the words of the immortal 1960's button A Mind, Once Stretched, Never Returns To Its Original Dimensions. The cyclist is in a position of power. The cyclist is not cooped up in a speeding box of sensory deprivation, but is still able to cover distances which takes them beyond the Local. The cyclist is not

Scarlet, aged 6

bound by the normal conventions of the pedestrian; social interaction, boring bits, a limited operating zone. The cyclist operates beyond normal limits, and consequently becomes alert, active, quick-sighted, keenly alive and responsible.

Hazards
Living Hazards
I have a book which tells you the best defence against attack by a) poisonous snake (wash with soap and water), b) shark (go for the eyes), c) bear (mmmm), d) alligator (even more mmmm), e) killer bees (run), and f) a bull (whip off the T-shirt and pretend to be a toreador). It does not tell you about farm dogs. So this is my theory. A farm dog knows you are not a sheep (it's no use pretending), ergo you are an intruder, ergo you need to be 'seen off', and your best defence is either a) speed, b) feign indifference, c) play for time with polite conversation, or d) aim a squeeze from your water bottle between the eyes. Farm dogs like to keep low (big clue for Spot the Dog competitions) so the worse case scenario is that it will wrap it's drooling fangs around your foot (rare). Most other dogs are too gormless to know you're there 'til you're gone (oops, come back dog lovers).

Midges and Mozzies. Glaswegians use raw lemon juice, the rest of us use Skin So Soft (ding dong Avon calling).

Last year I had my collar felt by a buzzard which then flew a metre above my head until I was well clear of the nest.

Hedgehogs. I have known a puncture caused by running over a hedgehog (dead).

Inanimate Hazards
Hedge Flailings. Hawthorn clippings and especially blackthorn can rupture your tyre however hard you pump them up. The flailing season in Wales is from 1st September to 28th February, beginning

a month earlier than in England, though who tells the fledglings that they have to vacate the nest by 1st September I have no idea.

Motorbikes. I used to ride one, a BSA C15, which got me to work (sometimes), but it was like a gnat to these big modern machines, and their riders like nothing better (where did this obsession with speed come from?) than filling up with petrol (with a time stamped receipt) and doing a 'run'. According to a 'source', the favourite Snowdonia runs are:

A4212 Bala – Trawsfynydd.

A5 Bangor to Shrewsbury.

A4085 Garreg – Beddgelert – Caernarfon.

B4393 Bala – Llanrhaedr-ym-Mochnant.

and Caernarfon – Llanberis – Betws-y-coed.

You can hear them coming, but remember that you are a blur rather than a serious impediment.

Motor Vehicles. My mate John has been cycling properly for 50 years, he's been thrown off 4 times, but put him behind the wheel of his Volvo and he's not the same person. Why? Impatience for one, distractions, the feeling of invulnerability, the fact that he hates driving, all make him a liability. If it was just John, you needn't worry, but there are thousands like him out there, and, in my humble opinion drivers are getting worse in their treatment of cyclists. You need to be vigilant, ride safely (see the cycling technique section) and reduce the risk. I'm not going to analyse the safety of individual roads, especially A roads, as many cyclists use these stretches every year without incident, but I have lost friends who were hit from behind by a car, or sideswiped, and it need happen just the once.

The Pan-Eryri Highway. Actually the A470 has been called many things, mostly uncomplimentary, though recent proposals include the Royal Welsh Way and the Owain Glyndŵr Highway, but it was cobbled together in the 1990's as a coast to coast highway,

Llandudno to Cardiff. I've mostly avoided it as a cycle route in this book, except for the only bits with a cycle path, around Llanrwst and Trawsfynydd, and through Manod and Blaenau Ffestiniog, where on-road parking means that it is faster on a bicycle. The 2 bits that are dangerous and difficult to avoid are the Bwlch Oerddrws (bwlch: *pass*; oer: *cold*; ddrws: *door*) from Cross Foxes to Dinas Mawddwy, and the short stretch from Llan Ffestiniog south to Cwm Cynfal, which is also steep and narrow. The latter stretch could be avoided by converting the defunct Blaenau – Trawsfynydd railway into a cycle track. What are we waiting for?

Bikes on Trains
Arriva Trains
Normally 2 bicycles are carried per train for free, but this is entirely at the discretion of the guard. On the north Wales line it is strongly recommended that you make a reservation (free). Tel: 0870 9000 773. On other lines, i.e. the Cambrian Coast line to Pwllheli and the Blaenau – Llandudno Junction line no reservation is required, but a first-come-first-served system operates. Most guards are very understanding.

Virgin Trains
Compulsory, free, advance reservations required, 3 or 4 bike spaces per train.

Welsh Highland Railway
There is a flat fare of £3, and most trains can accommodate a bike or two. There is a special waggon for large groups. Please book ahead. 01766 516024.

Ffestiniog Railway
A flat fare of £3 applies, but accommodation for cycles is limited.

Tal-y-llyn Railway
Aims to have space for 2 bikes on each train, but please give advance warning. The charge is £4 per bike.

A new National Rail Enquiries App provides quick and easy information on carrying bicycles on trains.

Snowdonia/Eryri

It is a land created by the elements, ice and rain and the sea, with a thin veneer of man and his sidekick, the humble sheep, which, with little apparent effort keeps the mountains naked and prevents a clothing of woodland from covering the land's modesty.

The Geology

Put simply the mountains are Silurian, Ordovician and Cambrian rock formed as marine deposits maybe 500 million years ago, and subject to much volcanic activity which pushed harder, igneous rock of lava into the other layers. The whole lot was pushed against the older Pre-Cambrian rock of Anglesey, and intensely folded (L. Dudley Stamp). Recent work in Japan following the tsunami has shed new light on the faults, shifts and slumps of the complex geology of Anglesey, and determined that the fault line which lies under the Menai Strait is the largest, most active fault in the UK.

The Geography

What you see now though is the result of glacial erosion; hanging valleys; cirques and cwm, morainic dams, pyramidal peaks and arrêtes; U-shaped valleys; the roches moutonnees of Llanberis; huge erratic boulders dumped by the retreating ice. All made by the frozen water you put in your G and T.

A couple of notable specific rocks:

The Great Orme is mountain limestone,

The slate is older than the volcanic mountain tops, and acquired it's personality from the intense pressure to which it has been subjected.

The National Park

After the Second World War in the late 1940's, the British Electricity Authority proposed the flooding of 5 Snowdonia valleys to create huge reservoirs for hydroelectric power; Nant Ffrancon, Nant Gwynant, Cwm Croesor, Crafnant and Cwm Penamnen. Megan Lloyd George, the MP for Arfon petitioned Parliament to await the creation of the Snowdonia National Park. The designation came in 1951. National Parks, though the name originally derived from a hunter's preserve, were intended as human sanctuaries, of the spirit through the power of natural beauty, and of the physical, the breathing of clean, fragrant and envigorating air.

Snowdonia National Park covers 826 square miles, is home to 26,000 people, with 6 million visitors annually. Welsh is the predominant language, the mother tongue of almost 60%. Traditionally the mountains in the north were known as Snowdonia, but the new boundary was chosen to cover an area which almost coincided with the ancient realm of Gwynedd, whose ruler by the mid C13th could call himself Prince of Wales. The Welsh name, Eryri, was thought, romantically, to derive from eryr, an eagle, but Mr Wetblanket, Sir Ifor Williams 'proved' that it simply means highlands. Controversially the designation left a 'Hole in the Park', Blaenau Ffestiniog, a very eloquent Hole.

A Bit More Background

45% of the Park is moorland, mainly privately owned sheep pasture, and another 30% is also in private hands. 16% is managed by the Forestry Commission now part of Natural Resources Wales, which formed the Snowdonia National Forest Park in 1937, covering 22,000 acres, including the forests of Gwydir, west of Betws-y-coed, and Beddgelert. The other huge afforestations are

Coed y Brenin and the Dyfi Forest, north of Machynlleth. The fractured nature of early decision making in the Park meant that further widespread afforestation, and the nuclear power station at Trawsfynydd, could not be effectively opposed.

The main employment sectors are tourism, agriculture and the public sector, with a net immigration of older people, and outmigration of the young, driven away by low wages and the high price of housing (14% are second homes).

A Touch of Controversy

The prime objectives in managing the Park are the conservation of the landscape and the advancement of biodiversity, and, you think, fine, nice words, but...

... to quote a Lonely Planet Guide, 'This is hallowed ground to both environmentalists and tourists, and the tension between the two form a major theme of the past, present and doubtless the future of the Yellowstone and Grand Teton National Parks.'

These USA Parks are older (designated 1872), bigger (about 4 times the size) and cater for half the number of visitors annually (3.6 million), and they are home to grizzly and black bears, eagles, lynx and mountain lions, but it is now agreed that the early management, weighted in favour of improving the visitor experience, was misguided and led to an unsustainable ecology, and that a more passive regime be adopted, favouring natural regeneration. Controversially, this included the release in 1995 of 14 Canadian grey wolves, resulting in the coyote population being brought under control and deer numbers reduced to allow natural regeneration.

If this logic were applied to Snowdonia, instead of trying to preserve the Park at a certain chosen time, with the landscape preserved in aspic by grant-aided sheep farming, it may be possible to move towards proper sustainability, both ecologically and economically. I am not expecting to see wolves in Snowdonia, but golden eagles would be great.

Management

National Parks were created to signal the Labour Government's commitment to access to the countryside, and chosen for their scenic value (termed 'conservation') and recreation potential. The 1995 Environment Act added a third purpose, the pursuit of social and economic wellbeing, designed to serve conservation and recreation, with funding provided to help and encourage this. A fine perspective on the challenges and appreciation of the National Park within the framework laid down by the legislation is available at www.snowdonia-society.org.uk.

The limitations of this framework have become clearer over the years. 'The unifying conception of... National Parks... was to ensure the preservation of rural landscapes and a rural way of life from the encroachment of urban sprawl and urban ways. The myopic reverence for this rural way of life ensured that precisely what it was that was being preserved was never examined too closely.' (Howard Newby, *Country Life*). The 'strict' preservation of the landscape produced land-use and landscape designations that were primarily negative with little attention paid to positive management or appropriate development. So we have a landscape pickled in a time of bald mountains, preserved by sheep, and conifer forests planted to strategically replenish our wood stocks after depletion in the trenches of the First World War. Preservation became institutionalised in the Planning profession at a time of social upheaval, and one consequence of this 'top-down' approach to the control of development has been the takeover of the countryside by the middle-classes and a resulting NIMBY attitude to change, except the change inherent in a car owning society.

Back in the 1970's the case was made for controlling access to the National Parks by car, but with one or two exceptions, any proposals were defeated by the power of the tourist industry lobby, and now it is never going to happen. But the price of petrol is set to rocket as we pass 'peak oil' and millions of new cars take to the roads in China and the Developing World, and there is sure to be a conflict between the nuts-and-bolts approach of the Planners and the need of local people to work out new ways of making a living, if the National Park is not to become a land of ghosts.

The Management Plan

The present management plan is – 'a varied and robust economy will be founded on environmental goods and services. These... will include agriculture... sustainable tourism... carbon sequestration, appropriately scaled power generation, building conservation and new opportunities for learning and understanding.'

I have a few quibbles:
- 'Sustainable tourism' means what, exactly?
- It is disingenuous to claim that 'power generation exceeds consumption', when the Park boundary is drawn to exclude the 100,000 people who live just beyond, and doesn't include the fuel in the vehicles of the visitors.
- None of our National parks have come up with workable ways to stop the loss of housing to second homes/holiday homes, nor to limit the swamping of the Parks with the private car.
- Hill farming operates at the margins of profitability, held together by CAP funding. This has recently been extended for 7 years until 2020, but it has been suggested that 'farmers are feeding from the public trough for the last time' (Tony Long WWF). In addition there is *Rhaglen Tir Eryri* (Snowdonia Land Programme). Begun in 2004 this uses EC funding of £4.35m. to help farmers and private

landowners 'restore landscape and historic features, enhance wildlife habitats and improve access'.

- It is suggested that future employment and 'sustainable' communities in the Park be linked to the environment, using the Park as an 'outdoor classroom', not only to learn about ecology, but also climate change and the role of carbon sequestration in the bogs. On a small scale *Bwrlwm Eryri* was launched in 2005 to 'maintain and promote Snowdonia's cultural heritage and landscape.' (*Bwrlwm* has been translated as a 'sense of place', but its meaning has far more energy and creativity e.g. a 'buzz').

It is hard to disagree with the thrust of the Management Plan, but I wish it were more radical, creative and honest. Do we want to turn the Park into an adventure playground or not? There is conflict, whether we recognise it or we don't. Witness the recent development of zip wires, inland surfing, underground adventures etc, and the call for 'something for the visitors to do when it rains'. Is this really the purpose of National Parks?

Tourism in Snowdonia

At the same time that Britain was losing the American War of Independence (or Rebellion as my mother-in-law called it), Thomas Pennant published his first *Tour of North Wales* (1778), beginning the popularisation of the ascent of Snowdon, with tourism given further impetus by the closure of the Continent to British travellers by the Napoleonic Wars, and it became fashionable to tour Wales on horseback or by horse-drawn coach.

A guide built a cairn on top of the Snowdon in 1820 and the Ordnance Survey raised a cairn in 1827. Guiding became popular and William Morris (an out of work copper miner) sold 'refreshments' from a stone shelter on the summit. By 1847 a small collection of wooden huts, known as Roberts Hotel and the Cold

Club had been built, owned by rival hotels, providing beds and beer. The first train arrived in 1896 and the Company took over the buildings and rebuilt, replaced again in 1935 by the Clough Williams-Ellis cafe.

During the last war my father stayed at a local hostel and 'walked' the Snowdon horseshoe, which meant shuffling on his bottom along some of the more precipitous bits, following a guy suffering from shellshock who pirouetted along as if he were Nijinski (the dancer not the horse).

Since the war the number of visitors has grown dramatically, and it is not unusual for 1,000 people to be on top of the mountain on a summer's afternoon. On 26th August 2013 walkers had to queue for 2½ hours to climb to the summit.

It is surely time to tip the balance away from the visitor experience and let the primitive environment reassert itself.

Fauna

A survey in 1958 showed that Snowdonia was full of foxes, otter, badger, stoat and weasel, and also pine marten (fairly widespread) and polecat (the principal remaining stronghold in Wales). Deer were virtually absent, instead there were feral goats. Voles, shrews and field mice were everywhere, also the red squirrel (fairly numerous). Stranded whales were not uncommon, including the Black Whale, and both porpoise and dolphin were numerous, the latter frequently coming into the Menai Strait. Of the birds special mention is given to chough, raven and peregrin falcon in the mountains, though by 1958 the golden eagle, although present in the mountains, had ceased to breed here.

Rethinking Time

You'll know, if you have read the companion volumes to cycling in Llŷn and Môn, that I was raised between the slag heaps of

Hatfield Main and the mires of Thorne Waste, and the glow on the horizon was not the rising sun but the Scunthorpe steelworks. So how come I'm writing a cycle guide to Snowdonia? Chance? Could be, but it also could be that my body has been possessed by the Spirit of the Age, who will use me as his/her voice. Goodness me, deep waters, dip your toe in if you dare.

We are unique, in this time and place, but only in the sense that every time and place is unique, and the footprint we make is added to the countless footprints which lie beneath, but because we have an unhealthy obsession with the here and now, we are blinded to the whole, which treats the past and the future and our own footprint in equal measure. Nuns at Quedlingburg prayed for the soul of Holy Roman Emperor Henry the First for nearly 900 years non-stop. On the banks of Llyn Geirionydd above the Conwy Valley is the Taliesin Monument, erected around 1850 by Lord Willoughby d'Eresby of Gwydir Castle on the supposed site of the birthplace of the C6th bard Taliesin.

Taliesin was granted immortality in the eyes of the people and his spirit sought a new body to inhabit (just as every promising cricket all-rounder is a new Botham), and he chose that of Gwion Bach from Montgomeryshire. But as a traveling spirit he inhabits all time and place, and it is with his spirit inside you that I encourage you to cycle these runs.

Historians use a time-line, suggesting a causal progression. If this were the true nature of time, then we would be able to predict the future, but really we know little of time. Kathleen Jamie (Sightlines) talks of an archaeological dig, of peeling back layers of time day by day, of allowing her imagination to visualise those dwellings one, two, three thousand years before.

A few oaks in Snowdonia could be a thousand years old, predating the slate quarries by 800 years, predating the estates, although we have them still because their situation in the landscape suited the gentry. We see the hand of the gentry (metaphorically only) in the slate spoil heaps and enclosed fields and grand houses, and so, as Jamie suggests, we have to stretch our imagination to find the lives of the ordinary in times gone by, as we pedal through their world. Perhaps, in this complex, detached, screen-saturated life, it is a stretch too far to see contentment or pleasure in a life lived in a damp, dark hut with most of the daylight hours spent splitting rock with simple tools, just as my own grandfather spent his working life underground working coal.

The difference is that though you can see the innards of the Earth pulled out and thrown discarded down the hillsides, the space you see between the rock faces, from one mountain to another, at some time that too was underground.

The Commons

Jim Crace in his 2013 book Harvest, points up the human cost of a landowner wanting to profit from land ownership, not only the human cost but the cost to wildlife too. If land is profitable then it has monetary value and if we decide that it needs to be preserved in some way for the common good, then we have to pay for it. This land, that was 'common' 200 years ago, i.e. ours, should we decide that it needs to be common again, we have to pay someone, perhaps even the family who took it for their own 200 years ago.

Now we are taking this a step further, with Defras Payments for Ecosystem Services, which decrees that we pay the managers of land and other natural resources for the 'benefits we derive from the natural environment', including woodland, clean air, fresh water, wetlands, moorland, mountains etc, i.e. we will pay 'service providers or landowners' for the 'guaranteed flow of ecosystem services', in essence for doing nothing, or, actually, for not destroying nature. This will be 'market based' using supply and demand which requires us to put a monetary value on a fresh water lake, an otter, a dragonfly.

(*www.gov.uk/government/publications/payments-for-ecosystem-sevices-pes-best-practise-guide*).

Garrett Hardin (The Tragedy of the Commons) back in 1968 pointed out that given the erosion of the 'commons' we have to do something to preserve it, but it seems to me a total abrogation of responsibility to give this to 'market forces', as if that were a perfect system for deciding the use of planet Earth, for not only are market forces massively skewed by public subsidy, for farming, energy production, tourism etc., but we humans have consistently failed to give any value to the ecosystems on which we depend.

Climate Change

I make no apologies for throwing this in, for any idea of preserving Snowdonia as it is, is simply daft.

'Climate change is the most critical issue that humankind has ever had to face. It is difficult to comprehend the scale of destruction we are bringing on ourselves.' Meyer Hillman with Tina Fawcett, How we can save the Planet. We know there will be more rainfall, warmer air holds more water, and more intense weather events as temperature differences provide more energy for storms.

Put simply, the increase in greenhouse gases began around 1750 and has been growing almost exponentially ever since. We can't switch this off even if we wanted to, but we show little sign of wanting to do so and are sacrificing the planet to save the economy. We have decided that a safe limit of greenhouse gases is roughly a third higher than at present, but we have really no idea what is 'safe', and are currently on course for a 5/6° rise in global temperature by 2100, roughly the same difference between now and the last Ice Age, and after that things will get worse. Long term studies suggest that each 1° rise in the global mean eventually leads to a 20 metre rise in sea levels, due to positive feedbacks, such as the increased heat absorption as snow and ice cover decreases and the release of methane from melting permafrost and drying peatbogs (*New Scientist*, Oct 2011).

In Britain the changes will be softened by the Atlantic. 'This will leave Britain and Ireland in a position that the rest of the World... will envy.' (Marek Kohn, *Turned out nice*). We will still need to conserve water, adapt to heat and respond to rising sea levels and the ecological balance will change, but the idea that we will be insulated against mass migration from uninhabitable places, from food shortages and political upheaval is ludicrous.

So Snowdonia will change, and our occupation of Snowdonia will change, for example, a key plank of the drive for Scottish independence is that it will become a mass provider of renewable energy and water to overheated England. The same will be true of Wales.

On an individual level our use of energy will be massively curtailed (probably by price) and, you've guessed it, this is where the bicycle comes in. Cycling is part of the solution. Look upon yourself as a pioneer. Though the idea that we will maintain the road infrastructure for a diminishing number of cars is also ludicrous. (Kingsley Dennis and John Urry, *After the Car*).

The Blaenau Ffestiniog ice cream van chime plays 'It's Now or Never'.

Flooding
Snowdonia and environs have been significantly affected by flooding in recent times, for example Llanrwst and Trefriw in 2004/5, Towyn (near Abergele) in 1990 when a storm surge caused 10m waves to break the sea defences and flood the town,

and the storm surges in 2014 which closed the railway to Pwllheli for several months.

Sea levels are rising, a little faster each year. Experts predict a rise by 2100 of between half a metre and 2 metres whatever we do now, with a higher rise than that a possibility because we don't know what will happen to the planet's ice caps (though scientists are shocked at the speed of melting, see the film Chasing Ice by Jeff Orlowski, 2012). With storm surges on top, as in December 2013, the rising sea levels pose a significant threat. If we burn all the fossil fuels on the Earth sea levels would rise by 72 metres, but it would take a thousand years or so (*National Geographic*, Sept 2013).

In north Wales we are planning for a 1 metre sea level rise by 2100, with a 20% increase in peak river flows. The places most at risk are the valley towns of Dolgellau, Bethesda, Llanberis, Machynlleth and Blaenau Ffestiniog; the coast at Tywyn, Barmouth and Porthmadog and the northern coast.

The plan for the Conwy valley is to reduce the canalisation and make more use of the flood plain to slow down flows.

Most work has been done on the northern coast, with concrete promenades and barriers in the towns, miles of 'dolos', twisted H-shaped cast concrete units (there are 22,000), and rock armour breakwaters and groynes. Rock armour (riprap) is the piles of large, heaped rock, designed to absorb wave energy, but it is not effective in storm conditions. You can still see wooden groynes, designed to capture and hold sand carried along the coast by long shore drift, but these are no longer considered to be effective, and are being replaced by beach nourishment, the mechanical pumping of sand from offshore back onto the beaches, though this is an ongoing process, not a one-off.

When you look at the plans for flood prevention and management, certain phrases keep recurring:

- 'We will continue to maintain our defences, but it may not be justifiable to replace them or to increase their height in future.'
- The plan is to 'manage the consequences of flooding.'
- The plan is for 'increased community and individual awareness.'

Cycling Technique and Maintenance

Cadence – It really helps if you learn how to ride a bicycle. Be aware of your rhythm, in cycling parlance, your cadence. Develop a natural flowing motion, timing and rhythm are key, like a Coleman Hawkins solo. Use your gears, that's why you have them. Focus on steady exhaling. The cardiovascular system transfers oxygen and other nutrients to our muscles. Any exercise which raises the heart rate and keeps it there increases the size of the heart muscle, meaning blood and oxygen are pumped more efficiently and your lungs have to work less hard.

Forget 'no pain, no gain'. Pain means injury. You may experience physical discomfort when you start, but not pain. Always listen to your body, it is the best friend you have.

Five Points of Contact

You have five points of contact with your bike, five weight bearing points. Avoid shocks to the arms with cycling mitts or with padding on your bars. The geometry of your bike is important here. Straight front forks improve handling but transfer jolts more readily, and the reason you have drop handlebars is not only to lower wind resistance when necessary, but to give you choice of riding position for long days in the saddle. Cleats or pedal clips keep your feet in contact with the pedals at the right angle, and help achieve more drive power on the uplift, though to be honest I've never been convinced this makes much difference. Practice ankling, so your toes move up and down with each stroke. If your knees hurt you are probably pushing too hard on the pedals, drop down a gear and keep your cadence higher. The fifth point of contact is the saddle. Where do I start? With Tour de France riders of old who used to cut holes in their saddles to accommodate the boils? I've talked to End to Enders who went through a jar of vaseline a day. I prefer a hard leather saddle, a Brooks B17, and if there is a problem an emollient cream (for nappy rash) like sudocream does the trick. My partner Annie is more sensitive. She rides with a sprung saddle and a sheepskin cover and will readily apply hanks of sheep's wool to the affected area if required. She has recently been given a gel-filled seat cover to try. Is this the same stuff they use for breast augmentation? It feels a little like tripe. The double gusset would be my luxury item if ever I were stranded on a desert island. But talk to your local bike shop, do not suffer alone.

Riding Along

I've passed bicycle hirers cowering in the roadside ditch, intimidated by cars pressurising their back wheels and hooting their horns. Let us get this straight, you have an equal right to be on the road as the fanciest of BMWs. The inequality comes when there is an accident or collision, a euphemism for a vehicle running into or sideswiping a bicycle. There is only one loser. So you need to ride defensively, and, against instinct, the best way of doing this is to be bright and bold. Take your place on the road and occupy it. Make vehicles overtake you properly when it is safe to do so, and not try to sneak by. Of course it helps the cycling fraternity if you help cars to pass when it is safe to do so.

In fact, take on board everything I've said here, and remember that you are a Superior Being. Just like the Queen, behave graciously, politely and confidently. Are you reading this John? And when faced with unfortunate minions, i.e. pedestrians, avoid the temptation to scare the living daylights out of them, by whistling, singing, sneezing or simply passing the time of day.

Maintenance

The essence of bicycle maintenance is 'little and often'. Use a proper spray-on bike oil, it lubricates without grease, therefore your chain will not attract bits of grit which interfere with the clean contact between chain and teeth and contribute to wear and tear. I usually spray the underside of the bottom bracket and chain stays to discourage the build up of debris and water which would eat at the metal.

Keep your eye on the brake blocks, replace when worn. The same goes for your cables. Keep your tyres inflated hard. Not only will this reduce rolling resistance, but it will help to discourage the penetration of your tyres by thorns. Years ago I carried a puncture repair kit, now I carry a spare inner tube, plus tyre levers and a spanner.

I am always learning. Wheels are fascinating things, apparently your weight is spread down through the spokes on your front wheel, but you hang from the spokes on upper part of your back wheel. Is this useful? It means your rear wheel is under more tension. Practice at home tweaking your spokes (I still use Richards Bicycle Book) so you can do this on the road if necessary.

Reflections on Space and Time

The wind which blows in your face is the same wind that blew when dinosaurs roamed, and the same wind that will ruffle the hair of your children's children.

Our western way of thinking is linear; the UK is a country of roads and cars, and always will be, therefore we must build more roads. To reach a destination we map out each step of the way. Our society is based on wealth and power and always will be. We are taught to climb the steps on the ladder.

The Zen approach to change is to agree a destination, locate the first step, then rely on flexibility and course-correction to reach the destination. The rhythmic view of time is longer, and can foresee a time when the car is in the trough of a wave and the bicycle is on the crest. Also the eastern 'destination' might be the 'arrière-pays', the place we can't quite see from where we stand, it's around the next bend, it's the place to which we are drawn as we travel.

A journey on a bicycle neatly encapsulates these two approaches. On the one hand there is the set route, sometimes numbered and named, '42', 'Lôn Eifion', 'Tour de France', with each step or stage spelled out. Another approach is that taken in Flemish Brabant, where you cycle from one node to the next, and at each nodal point there is a choice of 2 or 3 routes. A third approach is that of the anarchist, the cyclist heads off into the wind with no notion of a destination or route.

The one linking factor is that 'you are cycling on the 'Commons', you breathe 'common' air, ride roads on which no toll is charged, you pay nothing for fuel. The price of this ride is nil, but the value is so high it cannot be priced.

As a bonus, as you pedal, your brain is being plied with a steady supply of good oxygen, and yet you do not have to focus on a single task, your mind is free to wander, and when you stop for a panad (tea break), give a little thought to the wind and space and time, and the value we place on the 'mountain behind the mountain' and how we can best move in a time of change.

That's enough philosophising for one book. Whew.

Welsh

It has taken me too long to get to perhaps the most important bit. You are in the land of Cymry Cymraeg – the Welsh-speaking Welsh. Up on the moors, Welsh is the only language, for what business does an Englishman have up there?

At the time of writing (September 2014) a rather wonderful debate is taking place in Scotland, about the risk of becoming independent and the opportunity for self-governance. It is a debate which should be part of all our educations.

The Times' editorial on 12 September 1962 said 'the time has come for the Welsh people to free themselves from the shackles of the past and join the modern World by finally letting the language go'.

For a long time the struggle in Wales has involved the perception of colonisation and Anglicisation. The C13th conquest of Wales by the Anglo-Normans featured not only walled towns from which the locals were moved beyond an exclusion zone (even the Green Zone in Baghdad was home to some Iraqis), but also the selective imposition of tax and legal rights which made the Welsh subordinate in their own homes. In 1536 the Act of Union decreed that 'no person or persons that use Welsh speech or language shall have or enjoy any manner of office or fees'.

This is the song of all conquered people, it is not so much the coming, but that you stayed. And so, the infamous entry for 'Wales' in the 1888 *Encyclopaedia Britannica* read 'For Wales see England'.

The question remains, are the saving of the Welsh language and being 'masters of your own house' two sides of the same coin? The creation of the Welsh Assembly/Cynulliad Cenedlaethol Cymru has provided a platform for a movement towards a true bilingual nation, while recognising that the Assembly represents all who live in Wales, Welsh/English speakers or not. There is no doubt that prejudice remains on both 'sides', a laziness/ stubbornness in

English-only speakers, and its corollary, 'any language but English'. (Remember I come from Yorkshire, where we proudly drink from mugs declaring, in translation, 'You can always tell a Yorkshireman, but you can't tell him much'.)

It could be that the romantic Welsh stereotype is dead, and we have a clean slate and are growing the confidence to use it, both in the cultural and political Worlds. Perhaps the significant divides in Wales of north/south and urban/rural can be bridged, and inward-looking nationalism avoided by looking beyond the concept of a conquered nation to a European context, with Celtic connections or the recognition of City States. We must be careful to remove the rose-tinted spectacles though before hailing a new Welsh dawn. Many parts of Europe are undergoing fairly rapid and significant change; a polarisation between haves and have-nots (great chunks of Europe now have youth unemployment rates of 50% plus); growing immigration, both legal and illegal, from parts of the World under stress, and an unfortunate by-product, the rise of fascism. Where does Wales fit into a changing Europe?

The language issue is clearly mirrored in Pre-1914 central Europe, the melting pot of the Habsburg Empire, where a host of local languages remained for centuries whether you were, at that moment, part of the Holy Roman Empire, the Ottoman, the Magyar, the French or the Russian Empires, partly because local governance remained strong, but also because you lived your life as a 'local'. For a while, during industrialisation, the bilinguists held the cards, until nationalism and the corresponding Empire-building led us to war. Forced by the Scots in Britain (and the Catalans, Flemish and others in Europe) it seems to me that a similar process in reverse is taking place, as we tentatively move towards the internationalism necessary to reverse the destructive process of climate change which industrialisation set in motion.

Snowdonia is not isolated from these trends. As the Foot and

Mouth outbreak in 2001 showed, the economic importance of visitors at least matches that of farming.

The Welsh Language

Most of Snowdonia is Welsh speaking. There are parts, particularly in Caernarfon and the rural areas where Welsh is dominant, but fear not, it is one of the few places in Britain which is truly, and impressively bilingual. You need, however, to know about the pronunciation of the language. It is not simple, and for me the hardest parts are the vowels. It helps when Gareth Edwards says that Welsh is as easy as A B C (pronounced as in apple bog and cat).

Rules, or rather Guidelines
1) Don't panic, and don't jump in with a two-footed tackle. Betws-y-coed, for example is not 'Betsy Coyd' and Dolgellau is certainly not 'Dollygalloo'. Most place names break down easily. Penrhyndeudraeth = penrhyn (a headland) deu (two) draeth (beach<es>).
2) Pronunciation. The ones to watch are:
   ll. The subject of many a diagram involving tongue, teeth and lips. It is really only a problem if you don't have your teeth in.
   dd. A thick 'th'.
   ch. As in 'It's a braw nicht, the nicht', or if you are from Surrey, J. S. Bach.
   si. 'sh'

There are 7 vowels in Welsh.
   i. A long 'e' (the English 'ee').
   e. 'a' (as in day).
   u. 'i' (as in did).
   a. (as in hard).
   o. (as in pond or ore)

w. 'oo'.

y. On its own try 'er' sounding more like an 'a'. In the early part of a word it is a 'u', in the latter part an 'i'.

Also

f. is pronounced 'v'.

and ff is pronounced 'f'.

That's it, piece of cake.

3) Mutation. I love the idea of mutation, we do it in Yorkshire by omitting certain letters ('Ave yer no 'ome t' go t', 'Orsley). Welsh is a lyrical language, and to make it tinkle like a mountain stream certain letters can mutate. The common ones are p>b (pont>bont), b>f (bryn>fryn), m>f (moel>foel), c>g (cwrw>gwrw), t>d (tref>dref).

4) The adjective comes after the noun.
Snowdonia National Park is Parc Cenedlaethol Eryri.

There is some discussion about the language changing with the times, as does English ('train station' for Heavens sake!). Should a 'j' be admitted into the Welsh language for example (e.g. jĵns, jôc, jam, and half the population is called Jones – but this is English of course; John in Welsh is Siôn or Ieuan or Ifan or Ioan)?

And, lastly, there are discrepancies in the spelling of place-names between various editions of maps, road signs etc. This is partly due to the Board of Celtic Studies which pronounces on proper written Welsh, Betws-y-coed used to be spelt Bettws-y-coed, but mainly the Anglicisation of Welsh has yet to be fully worked out. Caernarfon, Dolgellau and Conwy have been rightfully restored, and, as far as I can tell, the corruption of Welsh place names in Snowdonia has not been as widespread as elsewhere. The once ubiquitous use of hyphens in place names has been reduced to the place-names which require a hyphen to ensure the correct stress when pronounced. Oh, did I not say, this should be on the second last syllable.

Proper place names only became necessary quite recently, with the introduction of mapping and postal deliveries. The naming of settlements after the chapel, Nasareth, Carmel, Bethesda etc came into use when the Post Office required a recognised address in scattered settlements, and the chapels were often in central locations.

Forestry and Woodland

Who would want to be a forest manager? The Forestry Commission was originally tasked with ensuring a plentiful future supply of props for use in coal mines and wartime trenches, with no thought given to the possibility upon maturity that there would be no call for either. This, of course, is a gross simplification, but managers have to work with a slow growing product in a fast changing World.

A) The Markets. In Britain timber grows relatively quickly, but is therefore less useful for construction or even telegraph poles, and more for wood pulp. But people read fewer newspapers and the digital age means less paper. At the same time supply is growing, Worldwide more trees are being felled. Timber suppliers have responded by cutting costs, 2 men and 2 machines now cut a forest, but management techniques are also moving away from clear fell and replant (and who knows how many replantings the degraded soil can take) to a more selective, coherent, sustainable system.

In the last few years a new generation of biomass power stations have been built (there are 8 in the UK, with a further 7 in the pipeline). It is obviously not a sustainable option to transport wood pellets around the planet, and there is deep concern that the Amazonian rain forest in Brazil is being used as a source, but equally we only produce at the moment about 10% of the wood pellets required. If Drax in Yorkshire were to operate at capacity it would consume 16m tonnes of wood a year.

B) Climate change is having an impact on our woodlands and forests as different species adapt differently to a warmer, wetter climate. There is a significant amount of research going on into the management of this problem.

C) Disease. Globalisation has meant the spreading of tree diseases all over the planet. Ash dieback is not the only ash disease imported from the east, an eastern beetle, the emerald ash borer is wreaking havoc on ash trees throughout the USA. Ash still grows in the Far East of course, for the trees there have learned to live symbiotically with the eastern diseases. As well as ash dieback there is sudden oak death and a dozen other diseases in the UK capable of killing trees.

The only solution is to work towards what the Woodland Trust call a 'resilient landscape', basically developing woodland with as many species as possible, of differing ages. Who knows, by the end of this century it is likely that, as the oil runs out, plastics will become expensive and we will once more look to the woods to supply tools and baskets and a host of other products once taken for granted.

Owain Glyndŵr

He was born into a Wales firmly under the English thumb, though these were unsettled times with King Richard the Second being a bit of a lad, and the country was ruled in a rather lawless fashion.

Owain trained in law in London and then fought for various English Lords, John of Gaunt (Henry's Dad), the Earl of Arundel and the future Henry the Fourth himself, before settling down on his estates in southern Denbighshire, minding his own business, not bothering anybody. Likely he would have died there had not his neighbour Reginald, Lord de Grey of Ruthin claimed a patch of his land, and using his influence with the newly crowned King Henry the Fourth, more or less had Owain outlawed. Owain was 41.

The flame of rebellion was lit. In September 1400 his supporters declared him Prince of Wales, and raising the standard of the red dragon, they invaded and burned Ruthin. Ravagings, burnings and reprisals followed, with Owain conducting guerilla warfare. Assisted by Henry passing penal laws against the Welsh, Owain soon acquired a supernatural reputation and led his rebels towards an independent Wales. Obviously, his own band of patriots/rebels wasn't going to be enough to see the job through, so Owain recruited Sir Edmund Mortimer (a claimant to the English throne) and married him to one of his daughters (I think we can safely say she was given little choice), also the Hotspur Percy, Earl of Northumberland, the Douglases in Scotland and even the French. He captured the castles of Harlech and Conwy, moving his household into the former, and opening a Parliament in Machynlleth, holding out until 1409. Afterwards his family were killed or rotted away in the Tower of London and the Welsh suffered reprisals. It was a land of poverty anyway, already ravaged by the Black Death, and once the flame had gone it was left to lick its bloody wounds.

Arguably the last truly Welsh revolutionary hero with the vision of a united Wales, the English stamped down hard following Owain's defeat (as they did in Scotland following the defeat of Bonnie Prince Charlie) and since then Wales has been clamped on to England. The country did not have a capital until 1955 when Cardiff defeated Caernarfon in a ballot.

Shakespeare referred to Glyndŵr as 'that great magician, damn'd Glendower', and for a while the mythology served both sides. That his reputation has endured is partly due to Thomas Pennant calling him a 'hero', echoed by the C19th nationalist dreamers, remembering his call for self-government.

No-one knows how, or where, or even if, Owain Glyndŵr died.

Edward Longshanks

Arguably, this English v. Welsh thing we can lay at the feet of Edward Longshank's invasion. So why did he do it?

We're talking 206 years after the Norman Conquest, but the English Royalty were still partly French. All the Queens in that period were French (Edward married two of them, the first, Eleanor of Castile was, unusually, a love match. She bore him between 14 and 16 children, most of whom died young, but when she herself died Edward erected 12 elaborate crosses at the places her funeral cortege stopped for the night. You can see the last one of these outside Charing Cross Station in London).

Edward's Dad was 'very fond of foreigners', appointing them to high office in England, much to the annoyance of the home grown nobles, eventually leading to civil war and in the final battle Edward defeated and slew Simon de Montfort. This set him on the path to 'embody the medieval ideal of kingship'. Edward (played by Patrick Mcgoohan in Braveheart) was big and intimidating with a temper and a lisp, and though he is remembered in Wales and Scotland as a hard-hearted tyrant, in England he was a reforming administrator.

Edward was crowned in 1274, but Llywelyn ap Gruffudd (grandson of Llywelyn Fawr) refused to attend, as was customary, on the very reasonable grounds that he had just discovered an assassination attempt by, among others, his own brother Dafydd, and here was Dafydd cuddling up to Edward Longshanks. Llywelyn also refused to pay the annual levy of 3,000 marks.

Edward was not best pleased, and launched his attack in 1276, based first in Chester, then in Rhuddlan castle. This he fortified and sent his troops around the coast to Anglesey, trapping Llywelyn in the mountains. By November 1277 he was short of food and submitted. The Treaty of Aberconwy allowed Llywelyn to keep the inner part of Gwynedd and his brother Dafydd (who had marched into Wales with the English!) was given overlordship of the land to the east of Afon Conwy.

But the English remained in charge of Rhuddlan and, according to Michael Senior 'behaved badly'.

Dafydd began the revolt. Llywelyn joined in, beseiging Rhuddlan. Edward moved north. Unfortunately Llywelyn was on manoeuvers with a select group when they stumbled into some English soldiers. One skewered Llywelyn without knowing his identity. Later, his head was cut off and put on display in the Tower of London. Dafydd was captured in 1283 and met a grizzly death.

Edward and Eleanor (Sophie Marceau in *Braveheart*) made Rhuddlan their home for a while as he set about subduing the locals. In 1284 the Principality was confiscated and made subject to the Crown, with an English framework of administration, and Edward had already begun to build.

Whilst on Crusade, in his youth, Edward had met Master James of St George, a Frenchman from Saint-George d' Espérance near Lyon. He brought him over and made him both architect and clerk of works.

He built Harlech castle, and the castles and bastide towns (self-sufficient communities of English settlers) of Conwy and Caernarfon all at the same time, costing £millions in today's money and employing thousands (you can imagine how much was subcontracted to the locals!). Conwy and Caernarfon took 4 years to build (1283-87), Harlech 3 years longer. In 1295 he began on Beaumaris, only to leave the castle unfinished in 1298. You're thinking – builders, ha, some things never change – but back home

Edward was having trouble raising the money (he taxed wool and Jews and seized church revenues) and also in persuading the gentry to keep him supplied with soldiers, oh, and in 1296 he invaded Scotland, defeating John Baliol but facing more determined foe in Robert the Bruce and Mel Gibson.

Meanwhile, back in England, the building of castles was against planning regulations (I kid you not), so they built cathedrals instead.

The Gentry in Snowdonia

The Civil War in Britain 1455–85, named by the novelist Sir Walter Scott as the Wars of the Roses, and renamed this Century as The Game of Thrones, was followed by widespread social disorder, not least because a high proportion of the nobility had met a sticky end. It fell to the Tudors to rebuild a class society based on strong local government, from the Sheriff (the Reeve, or magistrate of the Shire), and Lord Lieutenant (i.e. the Royal representative) down. All the officials were drawn from a local gentry made wealthier by patronage, intermarriage, acquisition and exploitation.

The importance and wealth of these landlords cannot be overemphasised. In Caernarfonshire in 1887 only 4.2% of holdings were owner-occupied, the lowest proportion in Wales, and half the land was in the hands of just 5 families.

Some of the Snowdonia Families and Landowners
The Penrhyn Dynasty

Richard Pennant (1737?–1808) was a merchant from Liverpool, already wealthy from inherited estates in Jamaica, and running the slave trade, when he married Ann Susannah, daughter of General Hugh Warburton and heiress to the Penrhyn Estate.

In the 1780's Richard, together with his steward William

Williams, bought out independent slate quarriers, appropriated Crown lands, and built roads and the Porth Penrhyn harbour in Bangor. Within 70 years the Penrhyn slate quarry above Bethesda was one of the largest in the World, employing 2,800 men, the income from which made the family one of the wealthiest in Britain.

His heir, his cousin George Hay Dawkins (1763–1840) expanded the estate, bought up most of the hotels in Bangor and built the enormous Castell Penrhyn. By the time George Sholto Gordon Douglas-Pennant took over in 1886, he was the third largest landowner in Wales with an immense fortune, entertaining Royalty in the castle on his rare visits, but he also had a reputation for unchallengeable authoritarianism and his arrogance led to the terrible quarryman's strike of 1900–1903.

The C20th saw the estate broken up to pay death duties, with the National Trust acquiring the castle and much of the remaining estate in 1951, and all family interest in the quarry was sold off in 1973.

The Faenol (Vaynol) Estate

Thomas Assheton Smith (1752–1828) inherited this Tudor estate in 1762 from his uncle, and, at the age of 10 became the third largest landowner in Gwynedd, the landholdings further increased by enclosing common land in 1806. He built a new mansion with proceeds from the other of the Worlds largest slate quarries Dinorwig, opposite Llanberis. By 1806 20,000 tons of finished slate were exported annually.

The estate was inherited by his son Thomas Assheton Smith Jnr., who was born in Westminster, educated at Eton and Oxford, where he was a prominent member of the Bullingdon Club, was a keen cricketer, Master of 3 packs of foxhounds in England, MP for Andover, then Caernarfonshire, but showed little interest in Faenol.

Subsequent heirs were far more convivial, enjoying their estates, particularly hunting and yachting. In 1884 G W D Assheton Smith built the 7 mile long wall around Faenol Park, with just 5 lodge gates, and within he roamed a herd of temperamental white cattle, deer and zebra. It also enclosed a zoo of exotic and dangerous animals. In 1904 the estate measured 36,000 acres with 1,600 tenants and G W D boasted he could walk the 15 miles from Faenol to the summit of Snowdon without stepping off his property. Charles Garden Assheton Smith (1851–1914) also trained Grand National winning racehorses here, including Jerry M, ridden by Ernie Piggott, Lester's grand-dad, in 1913.

The story last century matched that of Penrhyn, the estate being sold off in parcels, with the mansion finally being sold by auction in 1984 to a business consortium.

Glynllifon

The Glynne family had occupied the estate since Tudor times but it was further developed in the mid C17th with the marriage of Sir Thomas Wynn, a landowner in Llŷn, and Frances Glynne. Their Grandson Sir Thomas Wynn (1736–1807) was made an Irish peer in 1776 becoming known as Lord Newborough, and his son saw the rapid growth in slate quarrying by his Bangor neighbours, and, fancying a piece for himself, applied at the beginning of the C19th to 'enclose' the Uwchgwyrfai Commons, on the hills above the estate, including the small co-operatively owned quarries already operating there. With the help of Welsh lawyers in London he was defeated.

The estate, with its estate village of Llandwrog, and the 101 roomed mansion built in 1836–49, by 1873 comprised 28,800 acres.

During the Second World War RAF Llandwrog became the largest airfield in Wales, and the Royal Tank Regiment began training nearby, taking over Glynllifon, with Lord Newborough desperately trying to save his prize gardens from destruction by tank driven by Scousers.

In 1954 the mansion was taken over by the Council as a college and offices, with the house being sold on in 2000 as an hotel and wedding venue. The house was placed into receivorship in July 2013.

Contact between the estates was maintained by the Pitt Clubs. These were established in the C19th to honour the achievements of William Pitt, and celebrate his political principles by 'rousing the genius of the British Isles'. They did this with lavish meals, at which special silver-gilt medals were worn. There were 2 Pitt Clubs in Wales, the Pitt Club of Wales and the Menai Pitt Club, meeting in Caernarfon.

The Oakleys of Tan y Bwlch (Maentwrog)
The Evans/Griffith family trace their ownership of the Tan y Bwlch estates back to the C15th, and intermarriage with other local gentry kept things local until 1789, when Margaret Griffith married William Oakley, the son of a Staffordshire clergyman.

The estate village was Maentwrog, at that time the head of the navigable river, the quays on the river banks exporting wool, then slate, carried down the valley by pack mule from the quarries opened up at the beginning of the C19th around Blaenau Ffestiniog. William Oakley also built the church of St Twrog, the Dower House Glan William, and a new road down to Harlech.

Underground working at Blaenau began around 1840, with the Oakley Mine soon becoming the largest slate mine in the World, helped enormously by the opening of the Ffestiniog Railway line.

William Edward Oakley (1828–1912) did not get his hands on the estate until 1868, further developing the slate workings, rebuilding the Plas and adding new houses, a school and church in the village, which serviced the estate with a sawmill, blacksmith, laundry, Post Office etc. The oaks used in the Porthmadog shipyards came from Tan y Bwlch. Unfortunately the profligate son Teddy had no trouble at all spending the family fortune at his London club, and on the horses.

The estate finally evaporated in the 1960's and 1970's, though the house is now the study centre for the Park and much of the surrounding woodland has been taken back into estate ownership.

Rhiwlas Estate (nr. Bala)

Rhys ap Meredydd ('Rhys Fawr') led a group of men for Henry at Bosworth Field in 1485, and received in return land in Ysbyty Ifan and the Parish of Llanfor. In turn the land became part of the Price estate (from Flintshire) in the C16th. By the C18th most Merionydd landlords were absentee and the estates neglected, but at the beginning of the C19th the estates were noticeably wealthier and landowners began to invest locally in hotels and turnpike roads, taking advantage of the new tourism. R. J. Lloyd Price in the late C19th developed the 16,500 hectare Rhiwlas Estate as a shooting estate on the Scottish model, with pheasants reared in cages, keepers cottages etc, the clients either staying with him or in the 'Goat' in Bala. He also opened the Welsh Whisky distillery at Fron Goch, wrote books on pheasant, grouse and rabbits and introduced sheepdog trials to Wales.

R J was the father of Robert Kendrick Price, educated at Eton and Sandhurst and serving with 'The Buffs', and the father of the present owner.

By the late C19th Merionydd was largely owned by two men, R J Lloyd Price, and Sir Watkin Williams Wynn of Wynstay in Denbighshire (who was also the second largest landowner in Caernarfonshire). The people of Merionydd, strongly

Nonconformist, found it difficult to stand up to these landlords, and when they did vote for their own they were evicted from their holdings. It took two Reform Acts and a 'Peasants Revolt' before the son of a tenant farmer, Thomas Edward Ellis, was elected MP in 1886. His statue stands in Bala.

The Wynns of Gwydir (Vale of Conwy)
From the Statute of Rhuddlan in March 1284 to the Act of Union in 1536 the Conwy Valley was controlled by English colonial administrators. By 1536 'the Welsh gentry had proved themselves sufficiently sycophantic to be entrusted as agents of the English Crown' (Christopher Draper in *Conwy Valley Best Walks*, Carreg Gwalch)

After the Wars of the Roses Maredudd ap Ieuan ap Robert from Cwm Penamnen, higher up the valley, acquired the estate and began to develop the 'castle'. Sir John Wynn, First Baronet (1553–1627) inherited in 1580, developing the 36,000 acre Deer Park and, more importantly, cementing the family position within the Royal Court. He is known particularly for his influential History Book. The castle today appears much as it did in 1580 (at that time the quay on the river allowed access to some of the comforts in life, like wine and spices, imported from London).

The family cultivated their position and influence, and became 'the most important in northern Wales' but the estate was not as wealthy as the others and began to be broken up at the end of the C19th. The castle was sold in 1921, the contents auctioned, and following two fires, was abandoned until 1944. It is privately owned and undergoing restoration.

The Holyhead Road
Thomas Telford's Holyhead Road, being for the most part the

present A5 through Snowdonia, has been avoided where possible in this guide, though it is well used by road cyclists putting in the miles. Telford engineered the road with a maximum gradient of 1:22, and 'flattened' the bridges to avoid the road 'humpbacking'.

Remarkably the road is more or less intact, with many features, the walling, the road structure, the bridges, embankments and milestones surviving and in use today. Toll houses survive, at Hendre Isaf (NW of Pentrefoelas) and Lôn Isa (N of Bethesda) for example, the latter also having an original weighbridge housing and several 'sunburst' gates.

As the Waterloo Bridge in Betws-y-coed says 'This Arch was Constructed In the Same Year the Battle of Waterloo was Fought', and the whole road was used both as a celebration of the defeat of Napoleon and a showcase of the superiority of British technology. Thomas Telford was a Scot, from Dumfriesshire, as were many of the other notable engineers of the day (John Rennie, Robert Stevenson, MacAdam) and he was dubbed 'The Colossus of Roads'.

Telford was also responsible for the coastal road, including Conwy to Bangor, built for the Chester to Bangor mail coaches.

Movies in Snowdonia
Scores of films and TV shows contain scenes shot in Snowdonia. You will recognise the Watkin Path on Snowdon in Carry On – Up the Khyber, and Dot Cotton was an evacuee in Dolgellau. Clash of the Titans was largely filmed here, as was First Knight, with Camelot built on the banks of Llyn Trawsfynydd. The Bollywood actor Raj (Mayur Verma) lives in Dolgellau, and has plans, but the one to pull at your heart strings is Patagonia, filmed at Llyn Celyn, with the lost village beneath the waters.

Sheep

2013 The Results

You may not have heard that the Welsh Young Shepherd of the Year 2013 is 23 year old Rhydian Thomas of Rhydcymerau; the Wool Marketing board Personality of the Year is champion sheep shearer Gareth Daniel of Machynlleth; and the Sheep farmer of the Year is Keith Williams of Llandrindod Wells.

The Royal Welsh Show's Champion of Champions sheep went to Scotland, but Mr A Williams of Pentre, near Llwyngwril won the Llanwenog class. Llanwenogs are 'compact, black faced sheep with well sprung ribs and a strong loin and thigh', according to the National Sheep I. D. chart (www.nationalsheep.org.uk – everything from Badger Face to Zwartbles).

It is no wonder that sheep farmers need a subsidy for we are asking them to farm in a traditional manner, just as their fathers did, yet they themselves require a higher income to pay for their vehicles and computers, from the same flock. And who are we to begrudge them that? But the public subsidy means that the public therefore has a legitimate right to question this approach; to enquire about alternatives and ask what would happen if the subsidy were removed. All over Snowdonia there are remnants of lives which were not given public subsidy.

Key to sketch maps

Cyclepath/ Shared Path	- - - - ‾ ‾ -
Footpath	·· ·· ·· ··
Parking	P
Cafe	☕
Shop	S
Pub/ Hotel	🍺
Roundabout	◯
Church/ Chapel	✝
Camping/ Caravans	𝝠
Way marked cycle route	8

Caernarfon

A fitting place to begin. Caernarfon (the castle-in-Arfon) is Welsh through and through, and came second to Cardiff in a ballot in 1955 to determine the capital of Wales. It was already an administrative centre when Edward arrived in 1282, to make the town a key component of his conquest of Wales, building one of the finest castles in Europe, and a walled town in which he settled 60 English families. It is widely accepted that the town was modelled on the C5th city walls of Constantinople, built by Theodosius the Second to repel Atilla the Hun. I cannot do justice to the town here, really you should pick up a guide from the Tourist Information Centre. I particularly like the geological trail, the geology being the stones used by the different builders.

Cycling in Caernarfon

Sustrans Route 8 is signed into the town from Lôn Las Menai, through the walled town, around the outside of the castle, down past the Welsh Highland Railway terminus and on to Lôn Eifion. It is not easy to follow through the town as there is so much else going on, with the press of visitors and the remarkable townscape. My favoured route is to stick to the shore on the Promenade and past Victoria Dock/Doc Fictoria.

The town is incredibly easy to cycle out of. Not only is there Lôn Las Menai to Bangor, and Lôn Eifion south towards Porthmadog, but the pedestrian bridge over Afon Seiont leads you to the coast road, and just out of town Lôn Gwyrfai branches off from Lôn Eifion to take you into the mountains.

Cycling South
The Terrain
The coastal plain is a couple of miles wide, plus the tongue of sand, Morfa Dinlle, licking out into the Menai Strait. Crossing the plain are the rivers draining the mountains, Afon Seiont (from Llanberis), Afon Gwyrfai (from Rhyd-ddu), Afon Carrog (from Rhostryfan), Afon Llifon (from Moel Tryfan) and Afon Llyfni (Nantlle). The land rises to the mountains, becoming steeper as it goes up, until broken by the quarries on Uwchgwyrfai Common, as if the skin of the land had been slashed open and its guts were spilled out. It tops out at the great bulk of Mynydd Mawr (698m./ 2,300ft.), otherwise known as Mynydd Grug o'r Mynydd Eliffant ('elephant' Mountain).

The Cycling
Cycling on the plain is more or less flat. A cycle path has been created alongside the A499 from Llanwnda/Bethesda Bach all the way to Llanaelhaearn (see Llŷn Cycle Guide). The cycling lifeline for this patch is Lôn Eifion, climbing gently from Caernarfon to Penygroes and on to Bryncir (see *Llŷn Cycle Guide*).

To the east of this are dozens of small roads and tracks linking the old quarrying settlements, which obviously involve climbing, but the only severe gradient is the climb from the Snowdonia Parc Inn at Waunfawr onto the Common at Rhosgadfan. In the valleys beyond, the main climb is at Bwlchgylfin above Rhyd-ddu, and this is simply a steady ascent.

So this patch is perfect for loop runs of varying difficulty depending on your ability and inclination, though none are beyond the average cyclist, cycling the right way around.

Route 1 Lôn Eifion (Scarlet and Miss Pink)

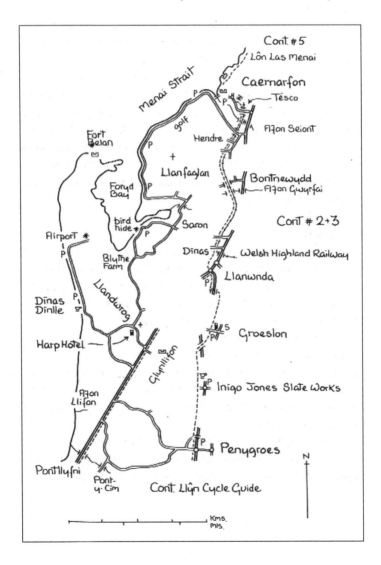

Route 1

Lôn Eifion (Scarlet and Miss Pink)

Run No. 1:   *Lôn Eifion (Scarlet and Miss Pink)*
Distance: *28k./17½ml.*
Grade: ₿₿

Take Lôn Eifion up to Penygroes. Come of at the footbridge over the bypass, turn right and follow the minor road downhill (branching off to see Pont y Cim if you wish). The wall on your right rings the Glynllifon estate. The A499 has a cycle path running alongside. The first left goes to Dinas Dinlle and the airport, the second to the Harp Hotel, Llandwrog. Turn right and follow this road to Blithe Farm, loop around the bay of Y Foryd, over Afon Gwyrfai and then left along the coast road back to Caernarfon. This is a popular sunday ride, you meet all sorts of cyclists from Miss Pink to the Beard on a Bike, Scarlet (aged 6) to the Cycling Pirate. Some have calves the size of marrows.

Pubs and cafes in Caernarfon and Penygroes, also pubs at Groeslon (Penionyn) and Llandwrog (Harp Hotel), and cafes at the Inigo Jones Slate Works, Glynllifon and Dinas Dinlle.

Plas Dinas, Bontnewydd
The holiday home of Lord Snowdon, the husband of HRH Princess Margaret, the Queen's sister. She had 'a penchant for late-night partying', he an undisguised sexual promiscuity ("If it moves, he'll have it" was the summing up of a close friend). All refs: Wikipedia.

Glynllifon
Llandwrog itself was the estate village for the Lords Newborough

of Glynllifon. The existing mansion was built 1836–49 and was, until recently, a Country House Hotel and wedding venue, with, in the grounds, a college, cafe and visitor centre.

Caernarfon Airport

The airport (museum and cafe) opened in 1975, using part of RAF Llandwrog, the largest airfield in Wales during the Second World War. It was built to defend Liverpool from Luftwaffe planes flying out of Brittany, then in 1940 the 'Warren' was offered to the 46th (Liverpool Welsh) Royal Tank Regiment for training, based at Glynllifon, and RAF Bomber Command used the airfield to train gunners and navigators. After the war, 71,000 bombs were seized in Germany, containing the nerve agent tabun, and stored here under primitive conditions until 1954 when they were dumped in the sea off Stranraer. A volunteer RAF Mountain Rescue team was formed in 1942, the precursor to the Sea Kings up at Valley (and soon to be privatized and re-sited back on the mainland). Many of the buildings remain, with new uses, including Parc Busnes Llandwrog and the antique shop at Blithe farm.

Fort Belan

Built by Thomas Lynn, Constable of Caernarfon to command the entrance to the Menai Strait as protection from raids by privateers during the American Revolution. It became part of the coastal defenses to protect Britain from invasion by Napoleon. It remains little changed.

Y Foryd Nature Reserve

Mud flats often alive with ducks and waders, especially widgeon. To access the hide ring 01286 67928.

St Baglan's church, Llanfaglan

An unrestored medieval church in the care of the Friends of Friendless Churches.

Pont y Cim

Pont y Cim is a packhorse bridge built in 1612, the year Shakespeare wrote *The Tempest*, and 5 years after the Gunpowder Plot.

Route 2 Tour d'Arfon

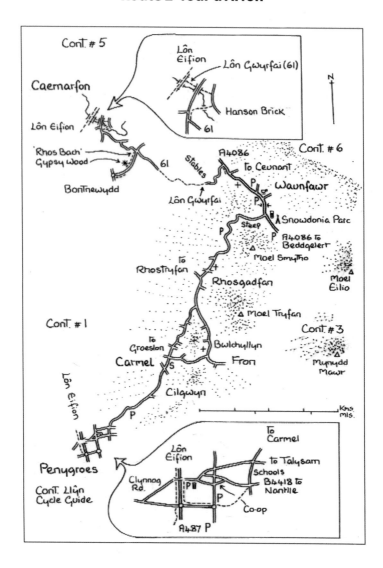

Route 2

Tour d'Arfon

Run No. 2: *Tour d'Arfon*
      Loop through the quarry villages of Cilgwyn,
      Carmel, Fron and Rhosgadfan
Distance: *26k./17ml.*
Climb: *110m./360ft.*
Grade: 🚲 🚲

From Caernarfon take Lôn Eifion to Penygroes, go over the footbridge, through the village and then up the road to Carmel. It's a steady climb, hemmed in by dry stone walls, with the World gradually opening up behind your back. From Carmel there is a plethora of small roads, but my preferred route is one of exploration, taking in Fron, Bwlchllyn and Rhosgadfan. From there follow the open moor towards Waunfawr, topping out at 260m./780 ft.. The descent is dramatic, steep and twisting, the valley side littered with erratic boulders, dropped by the retreating ice. Left at the Snowdonia Parc pub and brewery, and climb through the village of Waunfawr, then left on to 61 Lôn Gwyrfai, through the riding stables and it's a steady run back, on a hardcore lane to begin with, through twisting oaks, then on minor roads back to Caernarfon.

  Pubs and cafes in Caernarfon and Penygroes, also at Waunfawr (Snowdonia Parc Inn, home of Snowdonia Brewery, and the Blas y Waun cafe).

The Bypass
This is the place to mention the bypass. As I write it is still in the

Carmel

Cilgwyn

planning stage, with no route details published. The preferred route is from the roundabout at Llanwnda to the seaward side of Dinas and Bontnewydd, crossing the A487 with a roundabout about 2 miles south of Caernarfon, then looping to the east of the town to the big Felinheli roundabout. Costing £105m. work is scheduled to begin in 2015/16. The Active Travel Bill was approved by the Welsh Assembly in October 2013 and this requires that cycling provision be enhanced when constructing and improving highways.

The Quarries, Moeltryfan to Dyffryn Nantlle

The book to read is *The Quarrymen's Tyddynnod* by Dewi Thomas (Gwasg Carreg Gwalch 2005).

This is one of those places where a little knowledge goes a long way, and Dewi Thomas' book shines a light in all the corners.

To summarize – there is evidence of farming here back in the Iron Age, and by the Middle Ages the pattern of transhumance was well established, using cattle in the main, with the Hendre, the winter dwelling or home farm, down on the plain, and up on the slopes the Hafod or Meifod, the summer dwelling, with the cattle grazing the upper slopes.

Then came the Industrial Revolution and a demand for slates. The rock band here ran around the hillside from Moeltryfan to Cilgwyn to Dyffryn Nantlle, which the locals worked co-operatively, expansion bringing in other Welsh locals, rather than quarrymen from outside. But down below Lord Newborough looked up and fancied a piece of the cake (well, actually, he wanted the whole cake) and he followed the estates at Penrhyn and Faenol in applying to 'enclose' the common land for himself, including the quarries. He tried in 1804 and again in 1826, but was defeated with the help of Welsh lawyers in London, and so the seven quarries continued to be worked by locally owned small

Dyffryn Nantlle

Fron, above Nantlle

and medium sized companies from the early days in 1745 up to the 1970s, though The Welsh Slate Co. acquired Pen-yr-Orsedd in 2007.

The Commons were enclosed, but by the workers themselves, who raised Tŷ Unnos overnight, with smoke coming from the chimney by dawn. They then threw an axe into the four winds to claim the land for a small-holding. They were small, single story dwellings with a crogloft, and they were damp and cold and unhygienic. But the 'mountain wall' kept moving up the hillside, and when there was no more suitable land, 'tai moel' houses were built, houses with no land, and these became the villages. They were accompanied by shops, schools and chapels, and when the penny post arrived in 1840 and there came a need for an acceptable name for every locality, some of the villages were named for the chapel.

When men began to be laid off in the 1920s, the tyddynnod were slowly abandoned, with some of the men suffering from silicosis (slate dust) and tuberculosis, and people moved into the villages to be closer to the bus service to the factories in Caernarfon. Some are now ruins, others second homes, but it remains a place like no other.

Route 3 Into the Mountains

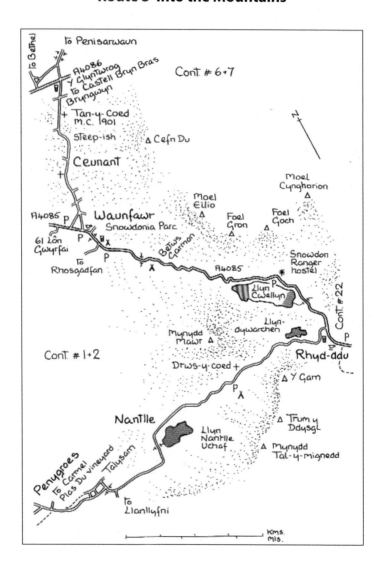

Caernarfon

Route 3

Into the Mountains

Run No. 3:	*Into the Mountains*
	Dyffryn Nantlle and Nant y Betws
Distance:	*35k./22ml. (round trip)*
Climb:	*70m./230ft.*
Grade:	🚲 🚲

This is a tremendous run, BUT don't do it on a Bank Holiday weekend. Pick a weekday in May or early June or at the back end of September.

The added loop begins at Waunfawr (see Runs 2 and 7) and takes you down into Nant y Betws, through Betws Garmon and past Llyn Cwellyn and the Snowdon Ranger Hostel. Snowdon looms like big Uncle Joe over Auntie Edie's sickbed. At Rhyd-ddu turn right and climb the 70m./230ft. to Bwlchgylfin, not a bad climb at all, up the pass at the head of the Nantlle valley. The run down is relatively short but lovely. Talysarn huddles among it's slate waste; follow the old road, which turns into a cycle path to the Plas Du vineyard (you did read that correctly) and on to Penygroes (see Runs 1 and 2).

For links to other nearby runs, it should be noted that there is in place a new multi-user trail from Rhyd-ddu down to Beddgelert. The main road is a fast descent, whereas the new section (opened Oct. 2013) is a relaxed amble of a path, mainly on forestry tracks with some rough bits and steep in places. It is also quite convoluted but waymarked (Lôn Gwyrfai signs on blue-topped poles). The scenery is spectacular.

Pub and cafe in Waunfawr (Snowdonia Parc and Blas y Waun

Llyn Cwellyn

Drws-y-Coed and Dyffryn Nantlle

cafe) and Rhyd-ddu (Cwellyn Arms and the Ty Mawr Tea Rooms), and the pub near Bryngwyn (Y Glyntwrog).

Penygroes

A 19th village built around the junction of Dyffryn Nantlle and the Caernarfon – Tremadog turnpike, which opened in 1810. Social housing and industrial estates have been added to alleviate the effects of the decline of the slate mining industry.

Antur Nantlle Cyf began in 1991 as a non-profit community business for Dyffryn Nantlle. It runs an Enterprise Centre with space for small businesses, IT training and Office facilities, and is exploring development opportunities for visitors and a possible mini-hydro electric power plant.

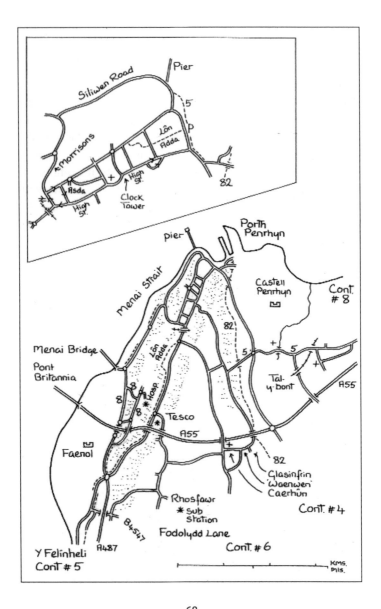

Pier
Siliwen Road
Morrisons
Lôn Adda
High St.
Asda
High St.
Clock Tower
5
P
82

Pier
Menai Strait
Porth Penrhyn
Castell Penrhyn
Cont. #8
Menai Bridge
Pont Britannia
Lôn Adda
Hoop
8
8
8
Tesco
A55
Faenol
82
5
5
Tal-y-bont
A55
82
Glasinfrin
Waenwen
Caerhun
Rhosfawr
Sub Station
Fodolydd Lane
Cont. #4
Cont. #6
Y Felinheli
Cont. #5
B4547
A487
Kms.
Mls.

Bangor

Cycling in Bangor

'Excuse me Sir,' I said to the policeman, looking up, 'can I cycle along the pedestrianized High Street?'

'No problem, fy nyn bach,' he replied.

The problem is, of course, that High Street/Stryd Fawr is one-way at either end, going away from the Clock Tower.

I think it is safe to say that the City of Bangor is not the best city for cycling, but it is by no means the worst, a crucial factor being the absence of cyclists. The University recommends that students NOT bring bicycles with them, and local groups know that until a 'critical mass' is achieved there are unlikely to be further improvements.

It is an easy city to leave with 3 Sustrans routes in place, small fairly traffic-free roads to the south, and a signed route Lôn Adda (Afon Adda being the culverted river in the valley) providing a fairly traffic-free route through the heart of the city and out to the Faenol roundabout. The roads are OK for cycling too, with just a couple of sections requiring extra vigilance.

1) Under the railway bridge at the beginning of Caernarfon Road. In my opinion cyclists should be on the road here, being part of the traffic, for the pavements are well-used by pedestrians.

2) The small one-way circuit in front of the railway station is no problem bearing in mind that at the traffic-lights by the station you are at the front of the traffic, and can therefore negotiate the 'weaving-zone' through eye-contact, bearing in mind also that a lot of traffic fails to 'weave' properly anyway.

3) Where the buses emerge at the mini-roundabout on Deiniol Road requires diligence.

4) Which brings me to Holyhead Road/Ffordd Caergybi from Upper Bangor to Telford's Bridge. Dual-use paths are marked

at the top of the hill and the bottom, but this footpath is so well used by students on foot that cyclists are a real nuisance. Why this road doesn't have a clear, segregated cycle lane I have no idea, and perhaps, as part of the £ multi-million Môn a Menai Sustainable Travel Area, it will get one.

From an entirely personal point of view I find that cycle paths like Lôn Adda can be frustrating; if you don't know the route you're looking for the signs, you have to watch out for pedestrians, children, dogs and your momentum is frequently broken. But I am quite happy cycling in cities. I learned the trade in Bradford in the 1970s; it is all hills; new, fast roads had been blasted through; winter rain and snow were the norm; the slots in rainwater gullies ran parallel to the pavements (!); and broken milk bottles were common (average 1 puncture a week). The 2 essential ingredients are:

- Eye contact, including eye contact through the drivers mirror. Remember that lorries, vans and buses have a blind spot when you are alongside. It is not a game of chicken. If there is conflict, you lose.

- Road positioning. Put yourself IN the traffic. It helps if you have reasonable acceleration from a standing start. It is rare that cyclists are run into from behind, most accidents occur when you are squeezed into a space which isn't there.

City of Bangor
Bangor is a University City. It is noticeable when the students are missing. It is not a wealthy city, the pedestrianized area has been described as 'Bangor during shopping hours is like a low budget zombie film' (bikeradar.com) and it has some of the worst buskers you will ever hear, but as a city it works (apart from Asda – why would anyone think that a free-parking supermarket in town will not affect the other shops?) and there are interesting buildings.

The Cathedral

St Deiniol built his cell and wattle enclosure in AD 525 (the word 'bangor' refers to the binding used in making wattle). Twenty years later he was given spiritual oversight of Gwynedd by King Maelgwn. St Dyfrig then consecrated him as Bishop, and the church was elevated to cathedral status.

The original wooden cathedral burned down in 634.

In 1073 the replacement was destroyed by Vikings.

In 1210 King John burnt down the next one.

In 1309 the new central tower burned.

In 1402 it was badly damaged during Owain Glyndŵr's rebellion.

Rebuilt 1496–1532 it remained intact until 1869, when it was renovated by Gilbert Scott.

Education

Friars School became a free Grammar School in 1557, having previously been associated with the Dominican Friary. Other theological colleges, St Mary's (Church in Wales) and Coleg Bala/Bangor and the Baptist Theological College, were late C19th institutions. The Teacher Training College was founded in 1858, the Normal College (so-called because the goal was to establish teaching standards or 'norms'). The University dates from 1884.

Other Buildings of Note

Bangor Pier. Opened in 1896, and restored 1988 virtually unaltered.

Old Bishops Palace. Originally built in the C16th, it houses the TIC.

Penrhyn Hall. Presented to the city by Lord Penrhyn in 1857, it is opposite the bus stands. During the Second World War the BBC Light Programme broadcast from here.

The circular 12-seater gents toilet, on the quayside at Porth Penrhyn.

Penrhyn Castle. Described on the one hand as 'a magnificent Neo-Norman Mansion', and on the other as 'a vast, grotesque monument'. Built 1827–36 by the Pennant family with a fortune made from sugar, slaves and slate.

Maritime connections
Shipbuilding

The C19th slate trade corresponded with a surge in shipbuilding along the Gwynedd coastline, creating much needed employment for craftsmen and crew. The ships, from small sloops to large brigantines, numbered in the thousands. In 1859, for example, Bangor had 4 shipyards, with Grampus, a 132 ton brigantine, 88 feet long, built at John Roberts yard. Rees Jones and Son in Felinheli (Port Dinorwig) built Ordovic in 1877, 853 tons, 168 feet long, a 3 masted barque. She sailed all around the World, being finally wrecked off Cape Horn in 1894.

With land transport in north Wales being so awkward, the sea was an easier alternative, goods being landed all along the coast on the tide by the small sloops, being finally superseded by the railways.

The Training Ships

In the C19th boys were taken to sea on ships to learn on the job, with onshore training given for those wishing to become master mariners.

In 1875 'homeless, destitute and poor respectable boys' of between 11 and 16 years were given training for the Navy and Merchant Service on board *T. S. Clio*, moored close to the Bangor pier-head. Clio was 211 ft. long, a 3 masted, 16 gun corvette, and took over 200 boys at any one time. They were fed and clothed, trained and disciplined (max. punishment 12 birch strokes) and sent to sea at the age of 16. The Clio was retired in 1919.

HMS Conway. In Liverpool boys were trained for the Merchant Navy on board the *Conway*. The third and final training ship was huge, a 92 gun battleship of 2,626 tons, formerly HMS Nile, launched in 1827. She was moved to the Menai Strait in 1941, moored first at Bangor then Plas Newydd, negotiating the Swellies in the process, with just 15 ft. to spare on either side of the ship. 12 years later the return journey, heading to Birkenhead for repair, proved to be her last and she foundered and wrecked in the Swellies.

Route 4 Lôn Las Ogwen

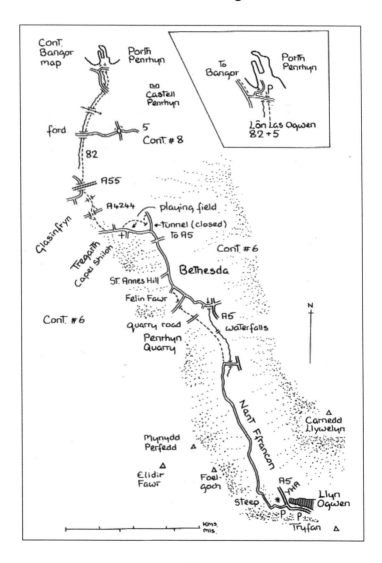

Route 4

Lôn Las Ogwen

Run No. 4: *Lôn Las Ogwen (82)*
Distance: *17k./11½ml. (each way)*
Grade: 🚲🚲

Slate has been extracted in Dyffryn Ogwen since the Middle Ages, but Lord Penrhyn, in the C18th combined the quarries, built the tramway to Porth Penrhyn and turned it into one of the World's largest slate quarries. The Quarry still operates, but the railway closed in 1962 and has been reopened as Lôn Las Ogwen, which then continues along the length of Nant Ffrancon to Idwal Cottage beneath the dramatic rock faces of Twll Du (the *Devil's Kitchen*).

You lucky Bangorites, through cuttings, over embankments and a viaduct, through woods and meadows and the slate quarry, and finally along the U-shaped Nant Ffrancon, it is hard to think of a more varied and dramatic cycle path.

Park at Porth Penrhyn and follow the metaled cycle path along the deliciously wooded Cegin valley. You hardly notice the incline.

At Tregarth it takes to the road for a short way past Capel Shiloh, then the cycle path continues through the playing field before stopping at a tunnel, forcing a short but steep road section at Pen-y-groes, then it's a mile or so on the Hen Durnpike to the outskirts of Bethesda.

Pick up the track again at Felin Fawr and follow the hardcore track through the workings. It is steep enough and loose enough for wheelspin, so I ended up walking a couple of short sections.

Above Pont y Ceunant, Lôn Las Ogwen joins the quiet,

Lôn Las Ogwen

Lambs in Nant Ffrancon

metalled valley road, providing marvellous views of the Glyderau, Clogwyn-Du and Tryfan. Spot the sheep marked with a red heart. The climb out of the valley to Idwal Cottage is steep.

Thinking of flying back down Telford's A5 to Bethesda? Think again. Traffic also thinks it can fly down here, but the bends make overtaking tricky. Leave this to the road boys and return the way you came, the thousand foot descent to the sea.

Pubs and cafes in Bethesda, and a new tea bar at Llyn Ogwen.

A slate fence near Bethesda with Penrhyn Quarry in the distance

Route 5 Lôn Las Menai

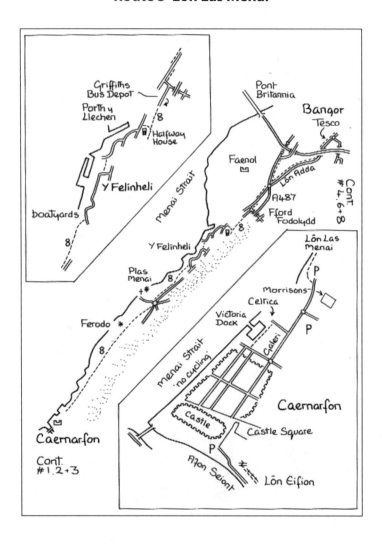

Route 5

Lôn Las Menai

Run No. 5:   *Lôn Las Menai (8)*
Distance: *12½k./8ml.*
Grade: ⚭⚭

From Bangor, reach the Parc Faenol/Vaynol Park roundabout either along Lôn Adda, or from Penrhosgarnedd, then follow the signs alongside the Felinheli road, picking up the old railway line at the B4547, past Griffiths bus depot to Halfway House/Tŷ Hanner Ffordd, then along minor roads at the dock, following these through Y Felinheli to the boatyards. Halfway up the hill pick up the old railway again and follow it to Caernarfon. You are never more than a field away from the Menai Strait, and the run is as straightforward as it can be.

Pubs and cafes in Caernarfon and Bangor, and Y Felinheli (cafe and Y Gardd-Fôn Inn).

Diversion Avoiding Bangor
Y Felinheli to Llandegai.
To connect from Lôn Las Menai (Route 8) to Route 5 (north Wales Coast), it does not make much sense to go into Bangor City, but to bypass on minor roads.

Leave 8 at the B4547 and take Ffordd Fodolydd, a steady climb on a rough, metalled single track road with more grass than metal, up to Rhos Fawr, Caerhûn and Glasinfryn, there to pick up Lôn Las Ogwen (82). Follow this north for a mile then take a left on to Route 5 (see Run No. 8).

I should mention that proposals have been mooted to re-open the railway line from Bangor to Caernarfon, which would drastically affect Lôn Las Menai. I think this is a pipe-dream, but you never know...

Ferodo factory
Opened in 1962 by Princess Margaret and employing over 1,000 to make auto friction components, e.g. brake pads. An industrial dispute in 2001 lasted 2½ years, and a while later the factory closed. Various proposals for a new use have been suggested, including a new prison, but the bill for clearing up the asbestos alone is expected to be £millions.

Route 6 To Pentir and beyond (1)

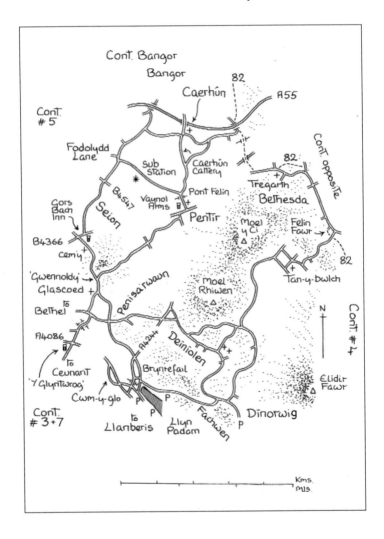

Route 6

To Pentir and beyond

Run No. 6:   *To Pentir and beyond*
            I Will Lift Up Mine Eyes Unto The Hills
Distance: *40k./25ml. (furthest loop)*
Climb: *240m./800ft. (Brynrefail – Fachwen – Dinorwig)*
Grade: 🚲 🚲 🚲 🚲

The other key to escaping Bangor on a bike is to head for Pentir, and you can do this in one of two ways:
1) Lôn Las Ogwen to the A55 overpass at Glasinfryn,
2) Climb the hill out of the valley either in town to Minffordd, or up behind the Tesco supermarket to Caerhûn.
     Pentir is easy to spot because of the Pentir (west Gwynedd) Substation.

A bit of a dog's breakfast this run, with a pick and mix thrown in. Basically you are doing 2 things:
1) Avoiding the roads with fast traffic. These are:
     – A4086 Caernarfon-Llanrug-Llanberis
     – A5 Bangor, Bethesda and beyond.
     also B4366 Llandegai – Bethel, which is used as an unofficial bypass.
     B4547, a link road to Llanberis.
2) Doing a circuit around the back of the 2 outlying hills, Moel Rhiwen and Moelyci. The road tops out at 400m./1200ft. and the circuit is marginally easier run anti-clockwise.

Route 6 To Pentir and beyond (2)

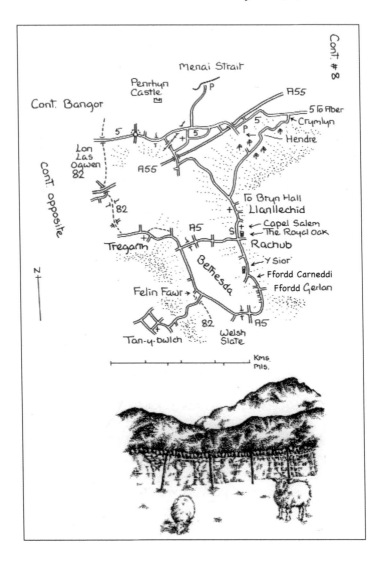

Cont. # 8

Menai Strait

Penrhyn Castle

Cont. Bangor

A55

5 To Aber

Crymlyn

Hendre

Lon Las Ogwen 82

A55

Cont. opposite

82

To Bryn Hall

Llanllechid

Capel Salem

The Royal Oak

Rachub

A5

Tregarth

Y Sior

Ffordd Carneddi

Ffordd Gerlan

Bethesda

Felin Fawr

N

82

A5

Tan-y-bwlch

Welsh Slate

Kms.
Mls.

Notes

The roads around Caerhûn/Pentir/Llanddeiniolen are quiet backwater roads through pleasantly undulating country. Up on the high point, Pen Dinas, the view of Snowdon is terrific.

The linking road to the runs out of Caernarfon goes from the pub Y Glyntwrog near Llanrug, up to Ceunant and down to Waunfawr. It is a stiffish climb up and over here, and in the process the character of the countryside changes to small-holdings.

The climb through Penisarwaun to Deiniolen is easier than that from Brynrefail through Fachwen to Dinorwic, though both are long, steady hauls, but that last bit up from Fachwen is a b---er.

The flatish moorland road up the top has you within spitting distance of the big mountains, and slowly the vastness of the Penrhyn Quarry is revealed. What on Earth is Tan y Bwlch doing up here?

From Bethesda through Rachub and Llanllechid is relatively easy cycling and you overlook a panorama of yachts and beaches on Anglesey.

Pubs and cafes in Bethesda, also pubs at Pentir (Vaynol Arms), Seion (Gors Bach Inn), Rhythallt (Y Glyntwrog), Deiniolen (Wellington Inn), Rachub (Y Siôr), and Llanllechid (Royal Oak).

The Grid

At the moment 3 high-tension electricity power lines carried on pylons meet at Pentir Substation. They are part of the National Grid. In addition power comes to Pentir from Dinorwig pump storage hydro station via underground cables, and from the Maentwrog and Ffestiniog hydro power stations. But change is in the air.

By 2016 a quarter of the power generation needed at peak demand in Britain will close (both coal and nuclear), hence the recent scare stories about potential blackouts. By 2020 the UK Government is committed to reducing carbon emissions by one third from 1990 levels (though, for heavens sake, both Japan and Germany seem to be abandoning their plans for carbon reduction!) The demand for electricity is expected to rise throughout this period.

To enable the switch to new low carbon generators (renewables and nuclear) new high-voltage power lines will be needed and this flow of power will be controlled from Pentir and from Trawsfynydd. The new nuclear power stations at Wylfa (3 are planned), and power from new offshore wind-farms in the Irish Sea will connect to the transmission system on Anglesey, which will also receive imported power from new Irish wind-farms and from the wave generating station near the Skerries. The existing system cannot cope.

The preferred solution is:
- A new overhead line between Wylfa and Pentir.
- Hanging a new line on existing pylons between Pentir and Trawsfynydd, including new underground cables across the Glaslyn estuary at Porthmadog.
- A new substation and pylon at Bryncir to provide power to Llŷn.

Deiniolen
Originally known as Ebenezer (the chapel was built in 1823 immediately prior to the first major phase of slate miners housing), this was first and last a slate workers village. 'The dire and evident poverty of this area reflects the social dislocation caused by the closure of Dinorwig Quarry in 1969. (www.heneb.co.uk). It is famous for the silver band, and as the birthplace of Dave Brailsford.

Huw Lloyd Edwards, Penisarwaun
Birthplace of the Welsh playwriter. The plaque is part of the writers plaques series, which also includes Brenda Chamberlain (Rachub) and R. S. Thomas (Bangor University).

Cefn Du Transmitting Station.
Between Groeslon and Ceunant Guglielmo Marconi built a large transmitting hall in 1914, last used as a climbing centre. Broadcasting commercial messages to north America from a long aerial suspended from 10x 400 ft. high masts on Cefn Du, the

station closed in 1939, and was used for the storage of bombs during the war.

Dinorwig and Snowdon

Bethesda

Route 7 Autopsy of Rock

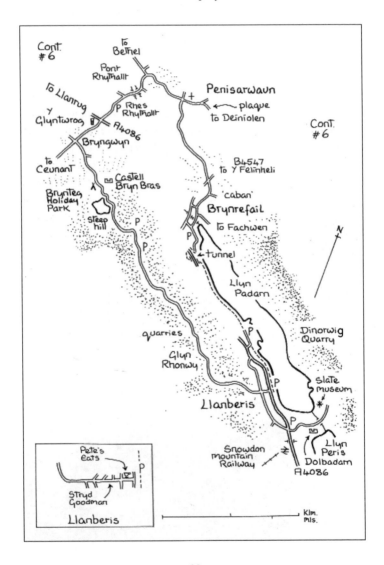

Autopsy of Rock

Run No. 7   *Autopsy of Rock*
             Llanberis – Pont Rhythallt Loop (Lôn Las Peris)
Distance: *18k./11½ml.*
Climb: *120m./400ft.*
Grade: 🚲 🚲

This shortish loop packs a real punch. Beginning in Llanberis climb straightaway up through the town past the Siemens factory and on into the heart of the slate workings. The innards of the Earth are exposed on all sides. Top out around 300m./1,000ft. at Pen-y-bwlch and from here the view is sensational.

It is a steep descent (which is why I'm running the loop clockwise) past Bryn Bras Castle and Brynteg Caravan Site to Bryngwyn. Right to Y Glyntwrog pub on the A4086, and on down to Pont Rhythallt. There's climbing again on the other side of the valley to Penisarwaun, left down a lumpy, single track metalled road, down through Brynrefail to the old bridge, where you pick up Lôn Las Peris. There's a bit of a shuffle to cross the A4086, then you're through a tunnel on the old railway line (good hardcore surface) and on alongside Llyn Padarn back to Llanberis.

The short Lôn Las Peris is an excellent Easy grade short Run.

Pubs and cafes in Llanberis, also at Rhythallt (Y Glyntwrog).

Llanberis

Llanberis is, and always was, a tourist town. The attractions; Snowdon Mountain Railway, Llanberis Lake Railway, National Slate Museum, Electric Mountain. Although the tourist route up

Snowdon is older (the mountain railway opened in 1896), much of the visitor stuff is more recent. There are plans too for another mountain bike centre over in the Dinorwig Quarry.

Castell Dolbadarn
Built in C13th at the heart of Llywelyn Fawr's kingdom (he reigned 1208–40). It was captured by Edward Longshanks, but survived as a Royal manor house.

Slate, Siemans and Hydro Power
The slate quarries are clawed out of Cefn Du almost to the top, but they are overshadowed by the mammoth undertaking across the lake at Dinorwig. One quarry, Glyn Rhonwy, was a major bomb storage depot in the last War, and was afterwards used as a disposal site, the bombs and incendiary units being detonated until 1975.

The Siemans factory manufactures reagents used on blood analyzers in hospitals Worldwide.

In the 1970s three million tons of slate were extracted from Elidir Fach to form the cavern for the pumped storage hydro-electricity power station (Electric Mountain).

Cwm-y-glo
Nitroglycerine (or 'blasting oil') was made in Hamburg and brought to Snowdonia in the ships which carried roofing slates the other way. In a scene reminiscent of the film Wages of Fear, two carts, each with a ton of the stuff, exploded after leaving Cwm-y-glo, killing 5, with debris spread over a square mile.

Route 8 Sustrans Route 5 Bangor to Conwy

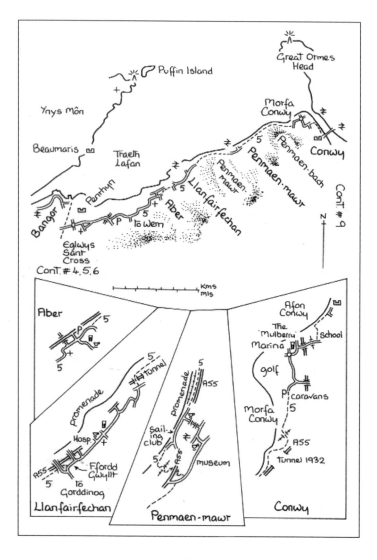

Sustrans Route 5 Bangor to Conwy

Run No. 8:   *Sustrans Route 5 Bangor to Conwy*
Distance: *27k./16½ml.*
Grade: 🚲

National Cycle Network Route 5 (blue marker with 5 inset in a red box) is a relatively traffic-free cycle route from Holyhead along the north Coast of Wales to Rhyl and beyond. This section covers Bangor to Conwy.

Route 5 leaves Bangor from Porth Penrhyn on Lôn Las Ogwen. After a mile or so, having ridden past the industrial estate and under the railway, exit to the right, come back over yourself and follow the lane towards the entrance to Penrhyn Castle. Shimmy around the roundabout then drop down into Tal-y-bont. Route 5 dances off to the right up to Eglwys Sant Cross, but it is 6-of-1 and a half-dozen-of-the-other whether to stay on the old road. Then it's over the new A55 and left at Hendre farm. It is 3 miles to Aber along a narrow, meandering, heavily-hedged lane, climbing slightly to Crylyn, though enjoyment is tempered somewhat by road noise .

From Aber there is half a mile of cycle path next to the speeding traffic, then you're off on the old road again through Llanfairfechan. Follow the signs carefully up a short sharply-rising road to a cycle bridge over the A55, then up a path over Pen-y-Clip headland.

In Penmaen-mawr Route 5 divides. Follow the signs down a convoluted path under the A55 onto the Promenade, or follow the road into town, down Paradise Road, then to the prom, under the road and rail underpasses, rejoining 5 at the cafe.

The next section is all off-road, but the path treads a fine line between the A55 and the railway. It is well used by cyclists (the next crossing through the mountains is way down at Capel Curig); around Penmaen-bach headland, over the new bridge, through the dunes at Morfa Conwy, eventually joining the road to the Marina. The signs take you over the A55, then left onto a shared path on the estuary side of Bodlondeb woods, and into the town at Lower gate Street.

The run is not a peaceful meander, but is never boring, with good views over Traeth Lafan (traeth: *sands*) to Ynys Seiriol (Puffin Island), then of the Great Orme and Deganwy harbour, and Sustrans deserve great credit for providing a safe route along this difficult coast.

Pubs and cafes in Bangor, Aber, Llanfairfechan, Penmaenmawr and Conwy.

Abergwyngregyn ('Aber')

The village grew from a medieval royal palace of Llywelyn Fawr/

Llywelyn the Great (the motte survives, in the grounds of Pen-y-bryn, a C17th house built in the Elizabethan style), built here at one end of the crossing to Anglesey/Môn. The 'road' across Traeth Lafan was marked with posts, and in foggy weather the church bell here in Aber rang to guide travellers to dry land. The channel, off Beaumaris, was crossed on a ferry boat.

St Bodfan founded the church in the C7th, the original church serving Llywelyn Fawr his own self. Some of the ancient yews were removed in 1878 when the present Gothic church was built. It is scheduled for a new use as holiday homes (the heads are thought to be of Saint Bodfan).

Aber's real claim to fame is the Aber Splash, the World's first railway water refueling trough, made in 1871 and in use until 1962 when steam engines met their demise.

Llanfairfechan ('Llanfair') (– the lesser church of St Marys)

A top-of-the-range holiday resort. Lancashire mill owners and merchants rented houses for the summer and moved their households here, including servants, back in the C19th.

In 1857 Oldham cotton magnate John Platt chose Llanfair for his country seat, buying the derelict Bryn y Neuadd, plus 150 acres, and enlarging it fourfold. He also bought Gorddinog and built an 'Elizabethan' mansion for his eldest. When John died the sons preferred the smaller mansion and in 1898 sold Bryn y Neuadd to St Andrews Hospital, Northampton to provide a care centre for 'lunatics and idiots'. In 1967 the hospital was reconfigured to care for mentally handicapped patients from north and mid Wales.

Penmaen-mawr (– head of the big rock)

Another holiday destination of choice, regular visitors included William Gladstone (see the bust, on Paradise Road).

The granite quarries opened in the 1830's and by 1905 granite was being shipped from the jetty at a rate of 1,000 tons a day. Its toughness makes it highly desirable for use in road building, including the German autobahn. The locals say, the lower the mountain, the more sunshine.

Off the coast is the city of Llys Helig, with a noted reputation for debauchery, which caused it to be drowned beneath the waves.

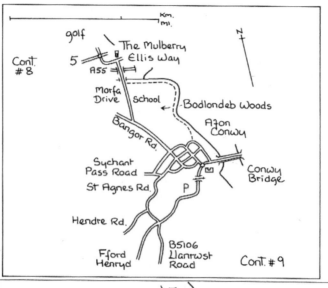

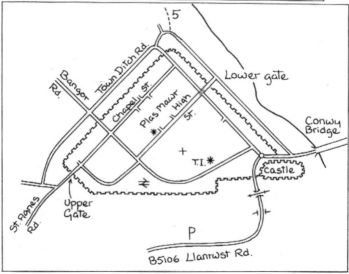

Conwy

Sustrans Route 5 is along the waterfront, continuing to Llandudno Junction and Deganwy across the road bridge. To cycle along the west bank of the Conwy Valley involves riding into the walled town, and choosing a gate to exit. In the town itself the roads are a grid, and the only thing you have to watch for are the one-way streets.

From Conwy there is, of course, a whole galaxy of cycling to the east, beyond the scope of this book. This includes Sustrans Route 5 along the coast towards Chester, and the Conwy Estuary Trail, an off-road cycle route from Llandudno Junction through Deganwy to Llandudno. Following a 12 month trial, cycling (informal and unsegregated) is now permitted along the whole length of Llandudno Promenade. For details of these routes pick up a cycle map from the Tourist Information Centres in Llandudno or Conwy, or online at www.conwy.gov.uk/cycling.

Could I put in a word for the run around Great Ormes Head/ Pen-y-Gogarth; a toll road for cars, but cycles go free. It is a one-way system starting above the pier in Llandudno, and there's a fair bit of climbing involved, but also a cafe half way around, by the lighthouse.

The Castle (World Heritage Site)
The castle was the most expensive of Edward's castles. Together with the town walls, it took 1,500 men four years to build, from 1283 to 1287. It was built as an English colony, serviced by sea, the Welsh being moved across Afon Gyffin to Gyffin itself. The castle was occupied in 1401 by Glyndŵr's forces, and hardly featured in the Civil War owing to its dilapidated condition. The Ministry of Works partially rebuilt the castle, which had also been previously altered by Thomas Telford (the 1826 suspension bridge

served as a prototype for the Menai Bridge), and by Stevenson, whose 1848 railway bridge was similar in design to the Britannia Bridge.

The present road bridge was built in 1955, and the tunnel in 1986, though I'm told that it is not a tunnel at all, but a tube laid on the seabed.

Plas Mawr, built in the 1570's by Robert Wynn, is now home to the Royal Cambrian Academy of the Arts.

The smallest house in Britain you'll find on the waterfront, with a chatty lady in costume.

The focal point of the town is still the waterfront, once a busy port trans-shipping goods from river traffic to sea going vessels. There were 4 shipyards. Several families still gather mussels in the estuary, now with PGI status.

Morfa Camp, beyond the Marina at the golf course, was used during the Second World War to build floating pier-heads, joined together to form a floating Mulberry Harbour, enabling equipment and personnel to be landed in Normandy.

Aberconwy Abbey. The site is next to St Mary's Church in the town. In the C12th Cistercian monks were granted this site by Gruffudd ap Cynan, King of Gwynedd (he was buried in the Abbey) and Llywelyn Fawr granted the monks extensive lands and privileges, worked by lay brothers who lived out in the granges. Cistercians were a hard working order, and so popular locally. Edward Longshanks moved the Abbey upstream in 1282 to Maenan, where it was looted by Henry the Fourth for supporting Owain Glyndŵr, and later vandalised by Henry the Eighth, the lands being 'acquired' by Elizeus Wynne of Gwydir.

Cycling in the Conwy Valley

Invaders from the east reached the bank of the Conwy and thought, aye aye, bit of a problem here. The banks rise steeply on both sides and the river occupies the valley floor in a series of S-shaped bends so beloved by geographers. Meaning, there's not much room for cyclists. The road boys choose the A470 on the eastern bank. Mostly it is wider and flatter but busier. The minor roads above the bank dash around, shooting up and down with dizzying and reckless ease.

The odd cyclist chooses the B5106 on the western bank. The trouble is, it's not actually a pleasant road to bike on, carrying a fair bit of traffic above Llanrwst, and being fairly narrow and waving, with hills. Vigilance is essential.

There is a weaving route on minor roads following the valleys of the rivers Gyffin and Ro, which is actually quite lovely to ride, and drops you on the B5106 at Caerhun. The run south from here through Dolgarrog and Trefriw is relatively flat, and from Llanrwst to Betws-y-coed the traffic thins markedly.

On either side of Llanrwst the A470 has been furnished with a cycle path, taking you (south) to the Capel Garmon road end at Hafod, and (north) to the minor road at Brynrhyd, to the south of the Maenan Abbey Hotel.

For this volume I'm limiting myself to two runs which venture into the National Park. For cycle runs to the east of this you'll just have to wait for the next volume, Denbighshire.

Pen y Gwryd Hotel

*Bwlch
Gorddinan,
Crimea Pass*

Nant Ffrancon

The Big Mountain Passes

I don't need to say much about cycling up these, you either do them or you don't. You share them with traffic (much greater in summer obviously), and many a road cyclist is riding as much for the computer readings as for the scenery.

All figures below are approximate (!)

1) Llanberis Pass (elevation 350m./1150ft.) A4086.
   From Pont y Gromlech in Nant Peris the climb is around 220m/730ft. in a mile, with a maximum gradient of 9%. From the Pen y Gwryd Hotel it is similar, 200,/660ft. in a mile, max gradient 10%.

2) Crimea Pass (elevation 385m./1250ft.) A470.
   From Blaenau Ffestiniog the climb is around 185m./610ft., but much of this is in the last half mile, with a maximum gradient between 15% and 20%. On the other side the climb is approximately 2½ miles from Pont y Coblyn, with a height gain of 205m./680ft., maximum gradient less than 10%.

3) Llyn Ogwen A5.
   It is a Telford road with a maximum gradient suitable for a coach and four. From Nant Ffrancon to Idwal Cottage the climb is about 100m./330ft. in 2 miles. From Capel Curig to Pont Rhyd Goch the climb is 120m./390ft.

Route 9 A Sunday Morning Jaunt

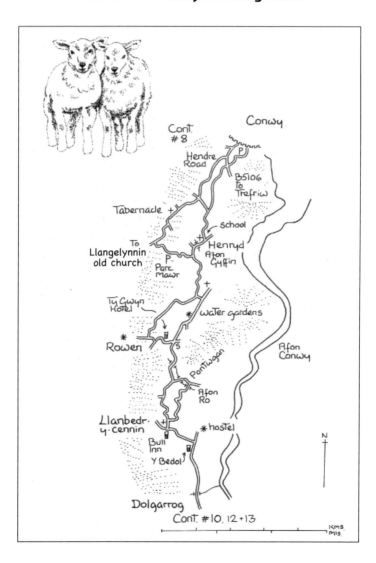

Conwy

Cont. #8

Hendre Road

P

B5106 to Trefriw

Tabernacle +

School

To Llangelynnin old church

Henryd

+ Afon Gyffin

P Parc Mawr

+

Ty Gwyn Hotel

* water gardens

Rowen

Pontwgan

Afon Conwy

+ Afon Ro

Llanbedr-y-cennin +

* hostel

N

Bull Inn

Y Bedol

Dolgarrog

Cont. #10, 12 + 13

1kms.
1 mls.

Route 9

A Sunday Morning Jaunt

Run No. 9:	*A Sunday Morning Jaunt*
	The villages of the Gyffin and Ro valleys
Distance:	*23k./14½ml.*
Grade:	🚲

From Conwy follow the route out through Hendre to Ro-wen and Llanbedrycennin, and back through Henryd, and you have a run in which the climbing is done on the way to the pub, and it is plain sailing home. The countryside is delightful, rambling lanes among old oaks and ancient hedgerows.

Frequent stops are a possibility as you reconcile the route on the map opposite, and reality in the flesh, as it were, but this is a jaunt, and not to be rushed.

To extend the route further involves using the B5106, down through Dolgarrog and Trefriw, and while this is not an unpleasant experience, the traffic forces you to concentrate on survival rather than float along the lanes like a fairy in Paradise.

Pubs at Ro-wen (Tŷ Gwyn Hotel) and Llanbedrycennin and Tal-y-bont (Bull Inn and Y Bedol).

Bryn Corach

Among the minor mansions around Conwy is Bryn Corach, built in a Scots-Baronial meets Conwy Castle style. It has been run since 1913 by the Holiday Fellowship to provide holidays for city dwellers. HF was founded by T. A. Leonard, and my great uncle Arthur Raistrick among others, part of the Socialist movement which also included the Independent Labour Party and the National Clarion Cycle Club.

Bodidda (in Hendre)
Built around 1550, the estate passed into the ownership of the influential Owen family.

Ro-wen
The village used to have 3 mills, a fulling pandy and lots of pubs. It still has one, Tŷ Gwyn Inn, and a YHA youth hostel.

Llanbedrycennin (– St Peter's church by the leek field)
The simple medieval church was restored by the Victorians.

The pub, Ye Olde Bull, a John Willie Lees house, used to be a drovers inn.

Ro-wen

Henryd

On Henryd Road used to be a tallow candle factory (made from molten animal fat), the candles being essential for the local lead miners. They carried the candles in a box with one open side, which gave them something to stand on to reach higher, and meant that the candles wouldn't blow out in a breeze.

Dolgarrog

British Aluminium opened a works here in 1907 using hydro electricity from several reservoirs in the hills above. In 1925 Llyn Eigiau burst its dam, the torrent overwhelming Llyn Coety and Dolgarrog village, with the loss of 16 lives.

Trefriw

Here were the wharves for loading the produce of the valley onto boats, lead, wool, and at its peak 16,000 tons of slate a year, for carriage to Conwy, where the goods were transferred to the sea going vessels. The railway put paid to the trade, and the town began advertising itself as 'the healthiest place in Wales'. In 1863 Lord Willoughby d'Eresby built a bathhouse below the old Roman spring. Ten years later a pump room was added, with the water proving, it was claimed, a cure for most things including 'brain fag'.

The paddle steamer St Winifred, and four other craft operated pleasure cruises from Conwy, delivering up to 1,000 visitors a day to Trefriw. After the Second World War the passage was billed as the 'Rhine of Wales'. The voyages ceased in the 1960s.

Route 10 Back in the Day (Gwydir Forest)

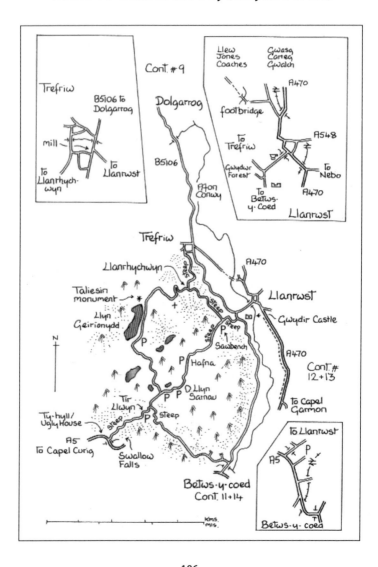

Route 10

Back in the Day (Gwydir Forest)

Run No. 10: *Back in The Day*
                Gwydir Forest
Distance: *15k./9½ml. (round trip from Betws)*
Climb: *300m./990ft.*
Grade: 🚲 🚲 🚲

Maybe it's the birdsong (they are loud, like they were auditioning for X factor) or maybe it's the sweaty men (they pop out unexpectedly, pumping away on their mountain bikes, seeming to make little progress uphill for the effort. They are chatty people, and you can have a whole philosophical discussion in the time it takes them to pass), or maybe it's just me, but it is difficult to imagine these hills throbbing with industry past. The ruins are there, and the holes in the ground. Would it have been as sylvan as it is now? Possibly, but charcoal would have been the main fuel source. Where did they live, these miners and smelters?

Right now this forest/woodland is a delight. Groups flow by, of walkers, off-roaders, plus the odd rambler exploring, and the hills to get you up here are a challenge. It is enough, really, just to be here, without pondering what it was like, back in the day.

The Run
Access the roads in the forest in one of 4 places:
1) Directly off the A5 at Tŷ Hyll (*Ugly House*), a steep 25% climb past the Towers Outdoor Ed. Centre.
2) In Betws-y-coed, off the B5106 immediately Pont-y-pair bridge over afon Llugwy. This is a lovely road through the

woodland/forest, with 2 steep sections bringing you out at Tir Llwyn.

3) The main access is near Gwydir Castle. 3 steep sections take you up to Llyn Sarnau. Part way up, a road to the right takes you to Llanrhychwyn, again this is steep.

4) From Trefriw a minor road takes you straight up to Llanrhychwyn, and, boy, is this a steep one!

So then you have loops to play with:
 – Llyn Sarnau – Llyn Geirionydd – Llanrhychwyn,
 – Llyn Sarnau – Pencraig – Betws-y-coed – Gwydir
 – Gwydir – Llyn Geirionydd – Betws-y-coed.

The B5106 from Betws-y-coed to Gwydir is a remarkably pleasant ride, tucked into the cleft between the valley floor and the steep hillside.

Llyn Geirionydd – Taliesin Monument

Wherever you go, this is lovely country for a road bike as well as a mountain bike.

Pubs and cafes in Llanrwst and Betws-y-coed, and at Trefriw (Old Ship/Yr Hen Llong).

Marin Trail
On of the UK's first generation MTB trails, the full trail is 25k. and described as 'difficult', but a 'true classic'.

Industry
There were slate quarries up here, but from 1850 to 1919 lead and zinc mining and smelting dominated the area, leaving a legacy of old engine houses, waste tips and reservoirs (used for power). The Cae Coch pyrites mine was a source of brimstone (sulphur) back in the early C17th. It was reopened in 1817, employing 100 men, and again in 1917 to service the War, with a power plant, compressors, a crushing mill and aerial ropeway. Is it time for another go?

Llyn Geirionydd
The monument was erected in 1850 by Lord Willoughby d'Eresby of Gwydir Castle for the C6th bard Taliesin, marking his birthplace. It was the chosen site of the annual Arwest from 1863 to 1927, a rival to the main Eisteddfod.

Immediately downstream was the Klondyke lead and zinc mine. Joseph Aspinal, a London socialite, bought the mine in 1918 and invested in its renovation. This was purely cosmetic, and included a cast of extras who leaped into action on hearing his car horn, to impress the visiting investors, often wealthy widows. Aspinal was found guilty of fraud in 1920 and sentenced to 20 years hard labour.

Gwydir Forest

Llanrhychwyn

Above the village is a medieval church, believed to be the oldest surviving church in Wales, and a place of prayer for Llywelyn ap Iorwerth and his wife Siwan. In a corner of the churchyard is a well. The parents of sick children came here and threw items of clothing into the water, in the hope that they floated. Sinking foretold death.

Gwydir Castle

The castle dates from the C14th, being rebuilt in 1490 by Meredudd ap Ieuan ap Robert, and added to in 1540 (with building materials from the dissolved Maenan Abbey) and again in the 1590s. It remains a fine Welsh Tudor courtyard house and is being restored, and open to the public. Known also for the gardens, with Cedars of Lebanon planted to mark the wedding of Charles the First in 1625, and the small gem, the C17th Gwydir Uchaf Chapel.

Lledr valley and Crimea Pass.

The Lledr valley has been described as the 'loveliest in Wales'. Unfortunately just about the only road in the valley is the A470; there are worse roads to cycle on, but it is not exactly pleasant.

The Crimea Pass (the road opened in 1854) is slightly less steep travelling south, though it has been improved recently at the Blaenau end. It is used by road cyclists.

Llechwedd

Next to the Caverns is the Stiniog MTB centre, a brand new £4m. investment with 4 trails, including a cafe, showers and a minibus uplift service.

Dolwyddelan Castle

Built by the father of Llywelyn ap Iorwerth (that's Llywelyn the Great) in 1170, Llywelyn was born here 3 years later. It remained a family stronghold until 1283 when Edward Longshanks captured and refortified the castle, although it was soon abandoned by the English, unable to supply the garrison by land (all the other castles have access by sea).

In 1488 it was purchased by Maredudd ap Ieuan, who made it his home. He also built the church of St Gwyddelan (noted for its rood-screen, box pews and fine pulpit). It is said that Maredudd moved to Penamnen to have safe access to the church, but his wife may also have had a say, and they soon moved on to Gwydir, and anglicised their name to Wynn (Wynne). Later the Victorians 'restored' Dolwyddelan.

Castell Dolwyddelan

Route 11 The Bishops Ring

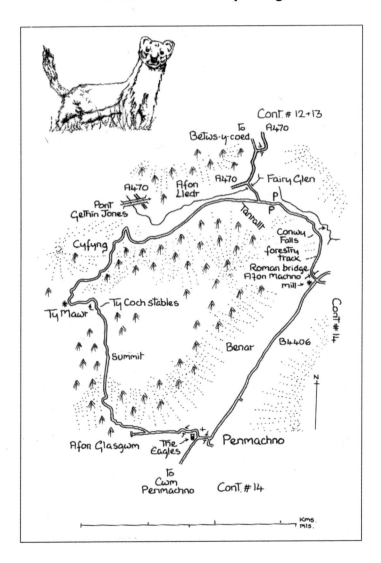

Cont. # 12 + 13
A470
To
Betws-y-coed
A470
Afon
Lledr
A470
Fairy Glen
P
P
Pont
Gethin Jones
Tanrallt
Conwy
Falls
Cufyng
forestry
track
Roman bridge
Afon Machno
mill
Ty Coch stables
Ty Mawr
Summit
Benar
B4406
Cont. # 14
N
Afon Glasgwm
The
Eagles
Penmachno
To
Cwm
Penmachno
Cont. # 14

Kms.
mls.

Route 11

The Bishops Ring

Run No. 11: *The Bishops Ring*
Distance: *12k./7½ml.*
Climb: *140m./460ft.*
Grade: 🚲 🚲

The road sign in Penmachno, by The Eagles, says 'Tŷ Mawr'. The climb through the pine trees is 140m./460ft., and steep, with mountain bike trails crossing now and then, but not much else. Over the top, the valley of Afon Wybrnant is lovely, and you cruise down past the riding stables to Tŷ Mawr, after which the road becomes an overgrown semi-paved track, which is also a delight. Towards the bottom you reach Cyfyng, and the old school and chapel for the valley. In the 1940s the attendance at school was around 40. Across the valley is the mighty railway bridge Pont Gethin Jones, a local builder.

After Tanrallt turn right onto a hilly, metalled road through woodland, climbing close by the Fairy Glen, then past Conwy Falls. On your left as you cross the bridge over Afon Machno is the Roman Bridge, probably a medieval packhorse bridge, and on your right is Penmachno Mill.

The B4406 is a pleasant valley road, then you're back in Penmachno. Notice the plaque for Richie Thomas (1906–88), one of Wales finest tenors, who turned down a professional career to remain in Penmachno; and the notice in the old shop for the Baby and Toddler Swap Shop.

Pub in Penmachno (The Eagles).

Baby and Toddler Swap Shop

Tŷ Mawr Wybrnant

The (rebuilt) birthplace of Bishop William Morgan in 1545. Chosen by the Wynns of Gwydir to be educated by their private tutors, he was then sent to Cambridge to study for Holy Orders, selected by Queen Elizabeth, he translated the Bible into Welsh Welsh in 1588, thereby ensuring that Welsh became the language of the new reformed Church in Wales. He was buried in St Asaph Cathedral.

Cyfyng, Nant Lledr

Penmachno

The church is Victorian but contains 5 early Christian tombstones dating from a time when the Romans occupied Britain. The font is C12th.

The valley was prosperous after the Wars of the Roses, as indicated by the 18 fine C16th/17th houses in which the small landowners lived with their servants and farm workers. The village was a focus for drovers routes, and a commercially important centre for wool. The Penmachno Woolen Mill began in the 1830s as a pandy, or fulling mill (rough cloth was beaten by hammers to matt the fibres) and remained a family mill (Hannah Jones and Co) until the 1960s when it became Craftcentre Cymru (now also closed).

The C19th saw the opening up of the slate mines at the top of the valley (Cwm Penmachno). These were part of the subterranean galleries used in the War for the storage of art treasures from London.

The Penmachno mountain bike trail is a community run venture, and begins just south of the village.

Route 12 The Golden Triangle

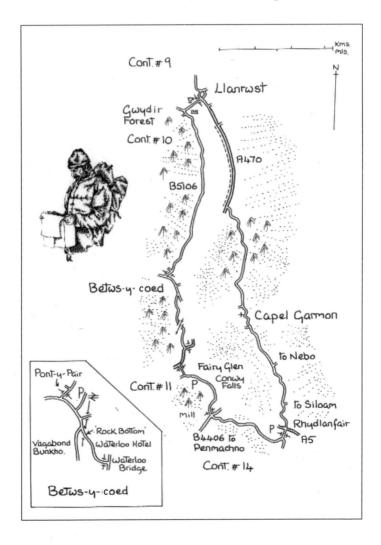

Cont. # 9

Llanrwst

Gwydir Forest

Cont. # 10

A470

B5106

Betws-y-coed

Capel Garmon

To Nebo

Fairy Glen
Conwy Falls

Cont. # 11   P

To Siloam

mill

Rhydlanfair

B4406 To Penmachno

P   A5

Cont. # 14

Pont-y-Pair
P

Rock Bottom
Vagabond Bunkho.   Waterloo Hotel
Waterloo Bridge

Betws-y-coed

Kms.
mls.

N

Route 12

The Golden Triangle

Run No. 12: *The Golden Triangle*
Betws-y-coed – Llanrwst – Capel Garmon
Distance: *23k./15ml.*
Climbs: *240m./800ft. from the north,*
120m./400ft. from the south
Grade: 🚲 🚲 🚲

Not, I hasten to add, that I mean to suggest that this is prime opium poppy growing country.

This is a comfortable, bountiful ride through luxurious woodland, apart from a couple of miles on a cyclepath alongside the A470 (Goodness me, this is a busy road), and then there is the hill. It is still luxurious country, verging on the picturesque, but the hill up to Capel Garmon, from either side, is steady climbing with steep bits (of around 240m./800ft. from the north, and 120m./400ft. from the south). Other than that, it's a doddle; balmy, almost.

Pubs and cafes in Betws and Llanrwst.

Capel Garmon

There's not much to the village, apart from the White Horse Inn, which has had an enviable reputation, but has been undergoing restoration for a couple of years now, and the Neolithic Burial Chamber, i.e. 5,000 years ago, a communal grave as fine as any in Europe from that period.

Route 13 The Promised Land

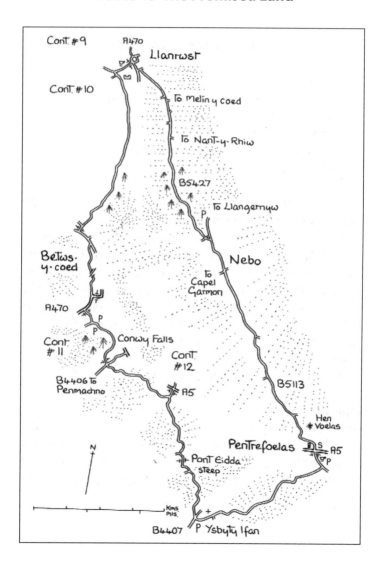

Route 13

The Promised Land

Run No. 13: *The Promised Land*
Distance: *36k./24ml.*
Climbs: *70m./230ft. : 100m./330ft. : 100m/330ft. : and*
120m./400ft.
Grade: 🚲 🚲 🚲 🚲

There is not much to Nebo, apart from the chapel, built by locals in 1813 and named after Mount Nebo, from which Moses was granted a view of the Promised Land. It is well named.

The Pentrefoelas – Nebo – Llanrwst road was the pre-Telford stagecoach road from London, and now forms the eastern boundary of the National Park. It is a rather pleasant ascent from Pentrefoelas up on to the Moor, with skylark, curlew and cotton grass for company. These are rounded hills, weathered by water rather than ice, indeed the big mountains seem a long way off, and so does the tourist traffic. It's just you, the farmers and the Tesco delivery van up here.

Between Llanrwst and Betws use the B5106, and the third side of the triangle makes use of the minor roads to the south-west of Afon Conwy; past Fairy Glen and Conwy Falls; over to Rhydlanfair; over again via Pont Eidda to Ysbyty Ifan, and these are quite steep ascents of 70m./230 ft. and 100m./330ft.; and over again to Pentrefoelas, another 100m./330ft of ascent.

I did mention the descent didn't I? A long ramp down a wooded hillside, the air full of birdsong, of around 320m./1,050ft. to Llanrwst.

Cafes and pubs in Betws and Llanrwst, and at Pentrefoelas the

Chocolate House and Tearoom, and the Foelas Arms, which used to be a posting inn on the Holyhead Road.

Pentrefoelas

'Foelas' refers to the motte or castle just north of the village, the castle controlling this route from England to Dyffryn Conwy. The old Voelas Hall, a home of the Wynnes, was demolished in 1819, but it is relatively easy to pick out some of the features in the estate village, the workshops, smithy, water mill and the farm buildings. The current Voelas Hall, alongside the A5, was designed by Clough Williams-Ellis and built in 1961.

Three miles east was the Prince Llywelyn Inn. It became a posting inn in 1808, with stabling for 69 horses, for this is the highest point, apart from Nant Ffrancon, on Telfords 1826 road.

The Levelinus Stone, now in the National Museum in Cardiff, was found near Hen Foelas. It is medieval, around 1200, and was probably erected by local monks to commemorate their patron Llywelyn ap Iorwerth. This was one of the main sheep grazing areas for the Cistercian monastery at Aberconwy. It is mainly a sheep area still. It was quite common locally for the farms to have

Nebo, near Llanrwst

small defensive towers, much as they did on the Scottish border with England.

Elis Prys

In the church at Ysbyty Ifan are the effigies of Rhys Fawr, the standard bearer for Henry Tudor at Bosworth Field in 1485; his wife Lowri, who owned the herb garden providing cures for the sick in the hospice of the Knights of St. John; and his son, Robert ap Rhys. Roberts second son, Elis Prys, was born nearby at Plas Iolyn in 1512. He graduated with a doctorate from Cambridge University wearing a red robe, hence his nickname, 'Y Dr. Coch', the Red Doctor. Thomas Cromwell appointed him one of the 'visitors' to the monasteries in Wales at the time of their dissolution, and his nickname began to take on another meaning. Elis Prys was a big shot locally, the MP and Sheriff, and he also became pals with Robert Dudley (Joseph Fiennes in the 1998 film Elizabeth), to whom Queen Elizabeth gave the Lordship of Denbigh in 1564. Elis Prys became a 'tool of oppression' in the hands of Dudley, and earned himself a reputation as 'the best hated man in north Wales'.

Betws-y-coed

In the C19th artists such as JMW Turner and David Cox were attracted here, to add to the local lead, zinc and slate miners and quarrymen, then the railway arrived opening up all sorts of other commercial activities.

Near to Pont-y-pair ('*the bridge of the cauldron*') over the Llugwy is a Rock Canon, 56 holes drilled into the rock, to be charged with gunpowder for an explosive fireworks display.

During the War both the Bluebird Cafe and the Waterloo Hotel were requisitioned by the Royal Army Medical Corps, with Coed-y-Celyn used as a Red Cross Auxiliary Hospital and rehab centre.

Route 14 Body Parts in the Sky

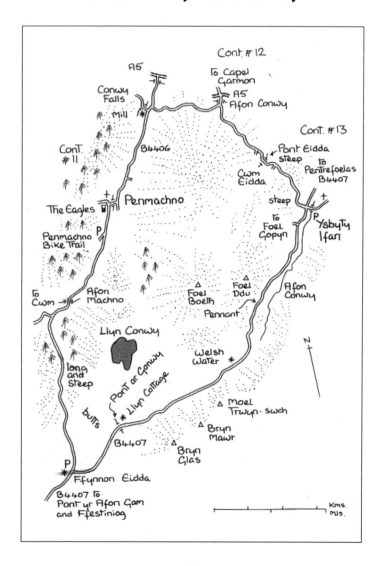

Route 14

Body Parts in the Sky

Run No. 14: *Body Parts in the Sky*
Distance: *30k./19ml.*
Climb: *275m./825ft.*
Grade: 🚲 🚲 🚲

The climb up the B4407 from Ysbyty Ifan feels like a secret passageway into the mountains, compared to most Snowdonia ascents, though every now and then the road rears up and nibbles at your muscles. You know you're gaining height for the trees grow shorter and scrubbier and then disappear altogether, and pastureland turns to rough grazing then to moor. As long as you're not fighting wind and rain, wide-open moorlands like this are quietly impressive, and in your idle moments you can spot body parts in the sky (oh look, there's a spleen).

From Fynnon Eidda to Cwm Penmachno is an immense plunge, and the valley road thereafter a delight.

The minor roads from Penmachno Mill to Ysbyty Ifan go up and over twice, the up bits being steep but short. You are riding up the side of a funnel as the water from miles around gathers to pour down to the Fairy Glen, but really these are little used waltzer-like roads and eventually you look out to Moel Seisiog, Moel Derwydd and Llynnau Alwen and Aled.

Pub in Penmachno (The Eagles).

The Migneint
Bog. Often the word barren accompanies bog, but this holds important reserves of mosses and ferns, and is also a carbon sink.

This was also a grouse moor for the Penrhyn Estate. Llyn Cottage (by the roadside) and the ruined lodge by the lake hosted shooting and fishing parties.

The National Trust, over the last few years, have built dams to block the estimated 300 km of drainage ditches dug up on the moor by post war sheep farmers, with the aim of improving carbon storage, reducing downstream flooding, especially in the Conwy valley, and enhancing biodiversity.

Ysbyty Ifan

The most prominent plaque celebrates Orig Williams 1931–2009, 'El Bandito'. He was the son of a local quarryman, a promoter of the Welsh language, but was best known as the professional wrestler fighting hard and dirty as El Bandito.

The village was known as Dolgynwal until 1190, then became Hospitium Johannes (John's Hospital – Ysbyty Ifan) when land was given to the Knights Hospitaller of the Order of St John of Jerusalem (the forerunner of St Johns Ambulance) by the local nobleman Ifan ap Rhys of Plas Iolyn, Pentrefoelas, impressed by the recruitment of 3,000 locals for the Crusades.

Following Edward Longshanks conquest in 1282, local law and order broke down and the hospice fell into neglect, but retained its right of sanctuary, so the area became a 'den of thieves'.

Rhys Fawr ap Meredydd of Plas Iolyn was the standard bearer for Henry Tudor at the Battle of Bosworth in 1485, and afterwards restored peace and prosperity to this area. Alabaster effigies of Rhys Fawr, his wife and son (Cardinal Wolsey's chaplain and cross-bearer) can be seen in the church.

Lord Penrhyn bought the Ysbyty Estate in 1856, primarily for the shooting.

The mill in the village ceased grinding corn in the 1930s, and for the next 30 years provided the village with electricity.

Linking Section: Afon Conwy to Bala

Back in 1951 the cartographers drawing the Park boundary came to this bit and said Time for a brew, closed their eyes and put pen to paper.

There is a direct way from Afon Conwy to Bala, via Pentrefoelas, Rhydlydan, Cwm Penamner, over Cadair Benllyn, Cwmtirmynach, Rhiwlas to Bala. It is roughly 21 km./13 miles, and involves 2 significant climbs, of 260m./860ft. and 235m./780ft.. There is not much up here but sheep.

A flatter route involves swinging up one side of the valley to Glasfryn, then up the other side to Cerrigydrudion (the A5 has a tiny footpath alongside. It is not scheduled as dual use, and not really fit for cycling, though we must make use of it from Cerrig to the B4501). The thing is, the B4501 actually takes a fair bit of fast traffic, notably delivery vans and wagons and canoe-topped cars heading for the white water centre. My mate John (he of the argumentative soul) refuses to cycle this way, saying it is too dangerous.

A wee bit further along, the A5 gives access to the network of minor roads in Nant Lleidiog/Dee Valley and on to Llandderfel and the B4391 to Bala. See the next volume in this series for details.

Bala

Bala has a comfortable, traditional feel. It has a cinema and a bike shop and no supermarket. People hang out, showing off babies and tattoos. It has statues and plaques galore (all men, I think). It has a leaflet 'bike routes around Bala' available from the nice man in the TIC (tucked away in the leisure centre – it seems comfortable with lower case lettering), and interestingly, 4 of the 6 routes are one-way. You almost expect to find clusters of cyclists at the destinations waiting for the leaflet 'bike routes back to Bala'.

The town goes back a long way. Roman chariots used the main street. The Tomen is a Norman motte, the castle of a Powys Prince. By the early C14th this part of the world was overrun by marauding bands of thieves, and Roger de Mortimer, the powerful Marcher Lord (home address: The Castle, Ludlow) in 1310 decided to get a grip and laid out the planned English-style town with 53 burgage plots and markets and fairs. Roger himself was a bit of a lad, being thrown into the Tower of London for insurrection, escaping by drugging the constable, fleeing to France, there to carry on a scandalous love affair with Isabella, the wife of King Edward the Second, finally being hanged at Tyburn by her son, King Edward the Third.

Two hundred years later Bala was a 'little poor market' (John Leland) and remained so, becoming a centre for shooting (pheasant, grouse) with a reputation for riotous fairs until 1791 when the powerful voice of Thomas Charles (statue: Capel Tegid) gripped the people with the harsh doctrines of Calvin, and Methodism swept the land. Lewis Edwards (statue, with chair) founded Coleg y Bala in 1837 as a College for Calvanistic Methodist Ministers. Opposite the College is a plaque informing you that here was a Congregationalist College whose first principal was the father of Revd. Michael D. Jones, founder of the Welsh republic in Patagonia.

In the C18th a cottage hosiery industry developed, producing, by 1830, annually, 32,000 dozen pairs of stockings, 10,000 pairs of socks and 5,500 pairs of gloves. Scarcely believable figures. The new turnpike roads brought staging post hotels such as the White Lion and the Royal, but one of the most 'colourful' buildings is the former workhouse. By 1869 it was a military barracks, then an oatcake factory and water bottling plant before becoming the Arran (Pyjama) Factory. It is now a shop, the PJs moving to Europe a few years back.

Route 15 Llyn Celyn (The Ghost Run)

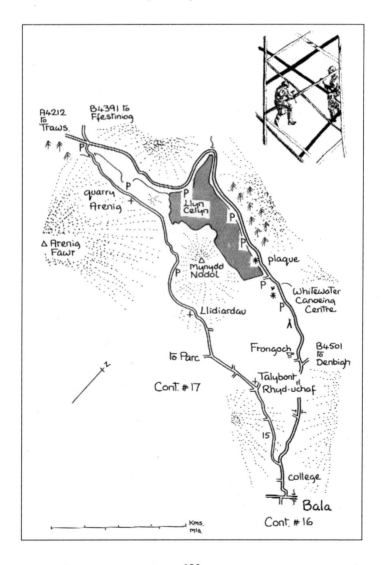

A4212 To Traws.

B4391 To Ffestiniog

quarry Arenig

Llyn Celyn

P

P

P

P

P

P

△ Arenig Fawr

△ Mynydd Nodol

P

plaque

Whitewater Canoeing Centre

Llidiardau

Frongoch

B4501 To Denbigh

To Parc

Cont. #17

Talybont Rhyd-uchaf

15

college

Bala

Cont. #16

Kms. Mls.

Route 15

Llyn Celyn (The Ghost Run)

Run No. 15:	*Llyn Celyn*
	The Ghost Run
Distance:	*28k./17½ml.*
Climb:	*210m./700ft.*
Grade:	🚲 🚲 🚲

The run from Bala begins with a head-down bottom-gear climb of 110m./365ft. to the marshy plateau of Rhyduchaf and Llidiardau. This is the land beyond, big rolling country with the song of lark and curlew and the mewing of buzzard. Behind you are the Berwyn (827m. high), to the left the distinctive peaks of Aran Fawddwy (909m.) and Benllyn, and ahead the ice scoured bulk of Arennig Fawr (854m.). The power line is part of the National Grid, striding over to Trawsfynydd, and, at the time of writing, the pylons are being painted by teams of men carrying paint pots and brushes.

The run tops out at 371m./ 1230ft. in a peaceful land of bog and moss, with only the buzzing of electricity for company. A little further on it

Pylon Painters

passes through the remnants of the village of Arenig before joining the A4212 at Ffridd Bwlch Llestri.

The simplest return route is back down the main road, which begins with a 30m./100ft. climb but then descends steadily, with some flats and false flats, back to Bala. The road is open and wide, traffic is not heavy but is fast and motorbikes do use it for speed, but generally it is a relatively safe downhill romp.

Pubs and cafes in Bala, and a cafe at Frongoch (Hen Siop cafe).

Arenig
A few houses remain, plus a converted zinc chapel and a powder magazine, used in the nearby granite quarry. Most residents worked there, plus a few railwaymen (Orsaf = Station). In the 1920s and 1930s between 30 and 40 secondary school age children caught the train daily to the school in Bala.

Llyn Celyn
The fate of the village of Capel Celyn in Cwm Tryweryn is still a pebble in the boot of many a local. The village, with its stone chapel and primary school was no different to many others, but in 1965 the village was drowned by Liverpool Corporation, along with 3½ miles of railway to make Celyn Reservoir (It is featured in the film *Patagonia*, 2010, with Matthew Rhys and Duffy). With a capacity of 16,400 million gallons, the water is drawn off the Dee 2 miles upstream of Chester at a rate of 65m. gallons a day, to flush the toilets of Liverpool.

Quaker Memorial
Near the dam (Pont Hafod Fadog) a plaque on a boulder marks the Meeting House and burial ground of early, C17th, Quakers. George Fox began the Society of Friends in 1652 and there are records locally in 1660 of their persecution, charged with failure

to attend church and refusing to take the oath of allegiance. George Fox was jailed all over England for refusing to remove his hat in Court. Many of these early Quakers emigrated to Pennsylvania.

Fron-goch

On the site of the school, in 1888 the Welsh Whisky distillery began production, then, in 1915 it was converted to a camp for German prisoners-of-war, and a year later, following the Easter Rising, 1,800 Irish rebels were held here, and it was here that the fledgling IRA gathered strength. In Ireland Fron-goch was known as the University of Revolution.

Route 16 Llyn Tegid (So near and yet so far)

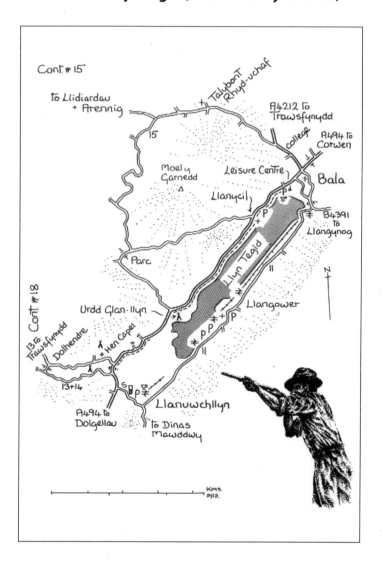

Cont. # 15

To Llidiardau + Arennig

Talybont Rhyd-uchaf

A4212 To Trawsfynydd

college

A494 to Corwen

15

Moel y Garnedd

Leisure Centre

Bala

Llanycil

P

B4391 To Llangynog

P

Parc

Llyn Tegid

N

Urdd Glan-llyn

Llangower

Cont. # 18

13 To Trawsfynydd

Dolhendre

Hen Capel

P P

13+14

S P

Llanuwchllyn

A494 to Dolgellau

To Dinas Mawddwy

KMS.
MILS.

Route 16

Llyn Tegid (So near and yet so far)

Run No. 16: Llyn Tegid
The 'So Near Yet So Far' Run
Distance: 22k./14½ml.
Grade: 🚲

This is a pleasant, picturesque run, relatively flat, beginning along the southern shore of Llyn Tegid on a quiet road, but with the Bala Lake Railway between you and the water, glimpses of the lake are few and far between. This run takes a totally superfluous but charming detour to Dolhendre, and returns via the A494 to Bala. Oh bother. This could have been an entirely pleasurable experience, not exactly enchanting, nothing to write home about, but pleasant, but the cycle path along the northern shore of Llyn Tegid has yet to be completed all the way along. A new 2 km. section from Llanuwchllyn opened in the summer of 2014, leaving just a kilometer or so past the Urdd and Glanllyn caravan site (phase 3). As yet there is no timetable for this, so you have to share the main road with Mansel Davies tankers. It is relatively narrow and close hedged, but not particularly busy or fast.

Pubs and cafes in Bala, and at Llanuwchllyn (The Eagles, and a cafe at the railway station).

Llangower
The church of St Cywair is C13th, heavily restored in 1871 and now in need of TLC. A rare 2-horse bier used to hang inside.

Bala Lake Railway

Operated with joy by enthusiasts. The Hunslet saddle tanks all worked the Dinorwig or Penrhyn Quarries and are all well over 100 years old.

Llanuwchllyn (– the church above the lake)

Birthplace of O. M. Edwards, author and scholar and his son Sir Ifan ab Owen Edwards, founder of the Urdd Gobaith Cymru, the Welsh league of youth. There are statues.

Dolhendre

The impressive Independent Yr Hen Gapel, dating from 1746, is being converted to a home.

Llanuwchllyn

Llyn Tegid/Bala Lake

The largest natural lake in Wales, formed after the Ice Age when the valley was blocked by moraine.

Gwion Bach left his home for Llyn Tegid, searching for Ffynnon Gwawr (St Gwawr's Well) which, by tradition, lies in a temple-city hidden beneath the waves of the lake, and protected by Tegid Voel, the C5th/6th chieftain. Among the many stories of Gwion Bach and his alter ego, Taliesin, of strange creatures and family ding-dongs, there underlies an ability to listen to the land and the water and hear what they have to say. (It has been said of John Wayne that myths are neither true nor untrue).

Llidiardau

137

Route 17 The Circumnavigation of Moelygarnedd

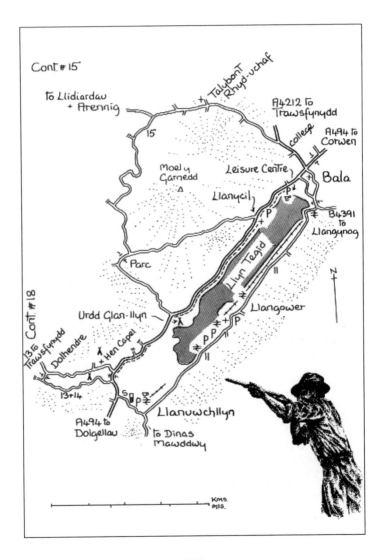

Cont. # 15

To Llidiardau + Arennig

Talybont Rhyd-uchaf

A4212 To Trawsfynydd

college

A494 To Corwen

15

Moel y Garnedd
△

Leisure Centre

Bala

Llanycil

P

B4391 To Llangynog

Llyn Tegid

Parc

Cont. # 18

Urdd Glan-llyn

Llangower

P

13 To Trawsfynydd

Dolhendre

Hen Capel

13+14

P

Llanuwchllyn

A494 to Dolgellau

To Dinas Mawddwy

Kms.
mls.

138

Route 17

The Circumnavigation of Moelygarnedd

Run No. 17: *The Circumnavigation of Moelygarnedd*
                 Bala – Rhyduchaf – Parc – Bala
Distance: *18k./11½ml.*
Climb: *140m./460ft.*
Grade: 🚲 🚲

Moelygarnedd is not the most exciting of peaks, in fact you hardly know it is there. It tops out at 360m./1180ft., and around the far side of the hill the run reaches 297m./980ft..

Leave Bala on the same road as Run No. 15. In fact this run is listed in the 'rides around Bala leaflet', being signed as 15. Follow the signs as it branches off left before you reach Llidiardau. The next stretch is like riding on a high shelf, between 200m./700ft. and 250m./800ft., firstly through tussocky moor and boggy grassland, giving way to grazing, the drunken road passes you on from one isolated farm to the next. From Parc down to the A494 the descent is steadily determined. There is a choice of route, but if you branch right, through Parc, there is a short climb out of the village of improbable steepness. The name Parc suggests the village itself is the product of the enclosures (parc = a piece of land enclosed by hedges).

Pubs and cafes in Bala.

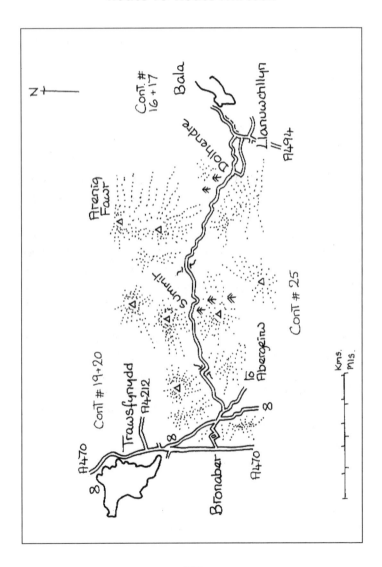

Route 18

Route Thirteen

Run No. 18: *Route Thirteen*
Llanuwchllyn – Trawsfynydd
Distance: *21k./13ml. (one way Llanuwchllyn – Trawsfynydd)*
Climb: *245m./735ft.*
Grade: 🚲 🚲 🚲 🚲 🚲

Don't be confused, this is Route Thirteen in the Bala cycle guide leaflet. The name says it all.

I wonder if many cyclists travel over here, all I've ever seen are sheep. It is not a spectacular route, but it is entertaining, and high, up to 531m./1752ft.. If you're not climbing, you're descending, and some of the climbs are really aggressive. There are also 6 gates to deal with, all on the Llanuwchllyn side. Here you are working up, following the valley side of Afon Lliw, the last farm being Buarth Meini. On the Afon Gain side, the upper reaches (Nant Ganol) are through a planted forest which at first sight is faring incredibly poorly. These trees were planted in a former MOD firing range, and you are warned not to leave the road. In preparation for planting special armoured tractors were used, unearthing 900 live missiles and 20 tons of dead shells. The tractor drivers were Honored by the Queen. In 2003 the sitka spruce was cleared and the area will be allowed to regenerate as broadleaf woodland. At Rhiw Goch you pick up Sustrans 82 (see Run No. 25).

Pub at Bronaber (Rhiw Goch Inn).

Blaenau Ffestiniog

Did I mention that I come from the south Yorkshire coalfield? We played on the slag heaps; we were told 'nivver go dahn t'pit lad'; and then the pits shut and that was it, but at least no-one drew a line around us and told us that our scarred face wasn't welcome. That is what happened to Blaenau, the Hole in the Park. There is a move to include it in Snowdonia National Park, to access extra support, at the expense of stricter planning controls, but in typical fashion the people of Blaenau have no voice in this process.

The town guide lists the things you can do here, fishing, canoeing, walking, climbing, singing, watching underground movies, dancing the samba. You have to look hard to find a mention of cycling: the Antur Stiniog Mountain Bike Centre (www.anturstiniog.com), and the proposed Velorail (a 'pedalo on rails' described as 'exciting', about which I think it is fair to say, opinion is divided).

For the ordinary cyclist there are better places. The town itself sits at 200m/720ft.. The Crimea Pass climbs to 385m/1250ft.; to the east the Migneint is 460- 485m/1500-1600ft.; and west all the roads drop to sea level. To the south there's a nasty bit of the A470 beyond Llan Ffestiniog, which would be easily avoided if, instead of a Velorail, a cycle path were installed on the old railway.

A Bit of History

In the 1760's Methusala Jones, a Caernarfon publican, opened the Diffwys Quarry, following a dream (bet his wife loved him, not only did she have to listen to his dream in the morning, but then he goes and carries it out). Getting the slate away was the real problem. At first the slate was taken out by pack mule, carried in panniers down to the boats on Afon Dwyryd, then trans-shipped in the estuary to sea going craft.

In 1836 the Ffestiniog Railway opened, followed by the LNWR line to Llandudno and the GWR line to Bala, and the town grew rapidly. Soon, of the 11,000 inhabitants, over 4,000 worked in the slate quarries.

Many of the high lakes were dammed to increase the headage needed for the water power below, to turn wheels, and later for hydroelectric power. Space was tight for the quarries, their workings, the tramways and railways and the huge piles of waste. In the Oakley slate mine were 50 miles of underground railway track in the bowels of the mountain.

The caverns were used 1940–1945 to house larger works of art from London's National Gallery, with specially controlled heat and humidity.

Today, with the population halved, and still falling, and the slate industry reduced to a rump, the town seeks a future. Artists such as David Nash and Falcon Hildred live here, and much work has been done to tempt visitors from the Ffestiniog Railway to tarry rather than bus straight up to Llechwedd. But, as I said at the start, I feel comfortable here.

Dolwen Power Station, Tanygrisiau

The reservoir was made in the late 1950's for the pump storage hydroelectric power station, in conjunction with the quarry tarn, Llyn Stwlan, above. It is, in essence, a way of storing electricity. The reservoir drowned the line of the Ffestiniog Railway, leading to the building, after a lawsuit, of the Deviation Line with its Alpine Loop, at Dduault.

Manod

High on Mynydd Manod are the granite quarries, including worker's barracks. Rock, and people, were delivered down from the quarries on four steep wagon inclines.

Llan Ffestiniog
Once a droving and trading centre, it was famous last century for Morris Evans Oil, at one time assumed to issue forth from a magic oil well, but actually mixed in a shed behind the petrol station. It was a cure-all elixir for both people and horses.

Rehau
The factory produces polymer plastics for the building trade, e.g. PVC-U windows and doors.

The Greenway Cycle Route
A cycle run from Trawsfynydd down to Dolgellau has been termed The Greenway, and is served by a shuttle bus on selected days of the year. See www.southsnowdoniagreenway.co.uk.

Route 19 The Head of the Valley Run

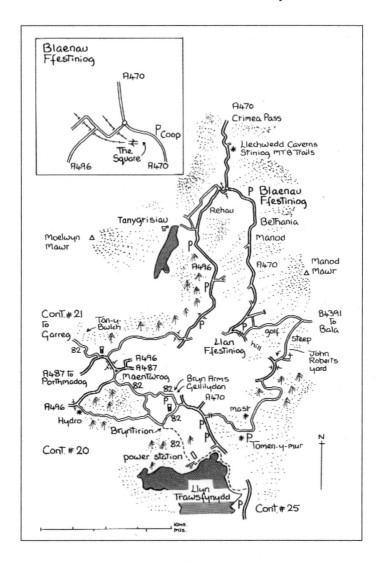

Blaenau Ffestiniog

Route 19

The Head of the Valley Run

Run No. 19: The Head of the Valley Run
Distance: 30k./18½ml.
Climbs: 210m./700ft; 80m./265ft.; and 100m./330ft.
Grade: 🚲 🚲 🚲 🚲

Beginning in Blaenau, this short but powerful run drops to Tanygrisiau, past the famous black sheep of Pengwern Old Hall, down to the valley floor at Pont Tal-y-bont, where you take the old road along the north side of the valley.

Plas Dôl y Moch is C17th, now an outdoor pursuits centre. Watch out for sheep and cats sleeping in the road. Pass through 3 farms, all with dogs, to Tan y Bwlch.

Over the bridge on the cycle path to Maentwrog. This was the estate village of the Oakleys of Plas Tan y Bwlch, and at one point a busy trading port for wool and slate, with quays, wharves and storehouses on the river banks. Note the huge glacial boulder by the parish church for which the village is named, Twrog's stone.

Route 82 takes the first minor road left, rising quite viciously (20% gradient) on this oak-lined lane. The next road along, from the Maentwrog Hydro (built in the 1920's and still going strong, unlike the nuke) also rises viciously, crossing the black snake of the pipeline towards the top of the climb.

The minor road chunters on to Gellilydan, past the new pub, then 82 takes to a mossy, oaken bridleway, rough in places, round to the back-end of the nuke (I haven't been this close to one since the protests of the 1970s). Then 82 takes on a jaunty air, less an alpha male route, more of a jokey amble, around the edge of Llyn Trawsfynydd through the fishing centre.

The track emerges onto the A470. The cyclepath and 82 continue right, but we need to get back to Blaenau. Going left, it is downhill on the A470. There is a footpath, but the cross kerbs are still stepped.

Take the first right on a minor road under a '9 foot headroom' sign on the railway bridge and climb again. To your right is Tomen y Mur. Then it's past the mast and an easy descent through forestry to the A470 and a short downhill run to Bont Newydd and John Roberts Yard. I'm taking you up and down on the minor roads to avoid the steep, narrow climb on the A470, though this lane is also steep. Down past the golf course, and a little shimmy in Llan Ffestiniog, then rejoin the A470 for the run back to Blaenau.

Blaenau Ffestiniog

Pubs and cafes in Blaenau, also a cafe at Tanygrisiau (Lakeside Cafe), and pubs in Tan y Bwlch (Oakley Arms), Gellilydan (Bryn Arms) and Llan Ffestiniog (Pengwern Arms).

Tomen y Mur

An important Roman military complex of which only the amphitheatre survives, as an earthwork. A castle was built on top of the rest a thousand years ago.

Route 20 Llwybr Llyn Traws Lake Path

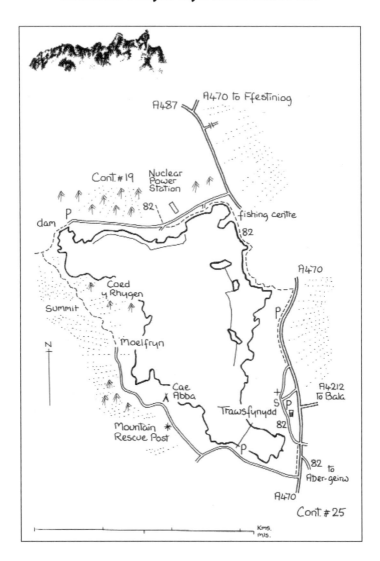

Route 20

Llwybr Llyn Traws Lake Path

Run No. 20:   *Llwybr Llyn Traws Lake Path*
Distance: *13k./8ml.*
Climb: *100m./330ft.*
Grade: 🚲

A brand new cycle path, completed in 2014 at a cost of £400,000, circumnavigates Llyn Trawsfynydd. I have a feeling that this will become popular. The country is quiet, attractive, full of bird song, with the Rhinog range marching away south, and, as the lady said as we caught her in-conveniently, 'I thought I was the only person for miles.'

The main car park is behind the Heritage Centre in Trawsfynydd village, and it doesn't really matter which way round you go. The section alongside the A470 is not pleasant, but safe, then you're on a lakeside path among Atlantic oaks emerging at the fishing centre. There are plans for bike hire here, but the chap I talked to rolled his eyes and said he didn't know when. Then it's the nuke. For a decommissioned plant waiting for half lives to halve there are an awful lot of worker's cars, and I suspect that decommissioning is behind schedule. The road runs through pines to the New Dam, for (of course) the Hydro power plant at the bottom of the hill still churns out electricity.

Then comes the climb, approx. 100m./330ft. on a steep, twisting hardcore path still rough in places as the bedding-in process continues. It is slow going but there are noticeboards and benches. From Moelfryn it is a flat tarmac road back to Traws. The footbridge is not convenient for cyclists as the wooden planks run lengthwise and wheels get trapped.

Keep an eye open for ospreys.

The pub is in Trawsfynydd (Cross Foxes Hotel).

Trawsfynydd ('Traws') (– across the mountain)
In 1928 25 farms were flooded to create Llyn Traws, to provide the power supply for the Maentwrog Hydro Power Station. The water was also later used for cooling water and as a heat sink for the nuclear power station, one of the first generation Magnox plants, designed by Sir Basil Spence, better known for the new Coventry Cathedral, though he was of the 'Brutalist' School of Architecture. The nuke is now being decommissioned, the nuclear fuel removed and the reactors 'made safe', though it will be 100 years before the buildings can be safely demolished. Land around the power station is scheduled for use as a business enterprise zone.

A report in 2006 suggested that the raised levels of cancer in the vicinity could be caused by the nuclear plant, but they could also be a result of the fallout in the Chernobyl rain in 1986. Restrictions on sheep from the area were finally lifted in 2012.

Capel Moriah dominates the village itself. The Llys Ednowain Hostel, adjacent to the Heritage Centre, used to be the Temperance Hotel for the officers from Bronaber. The statue is Hedd Wyn, the bard, tragically killed at Passchendaele.

Bronaber
In 1906 a military camp was set up at Rhiw Goch (now the hotel), expanded during WW1 to include an artillery range and POW camp. Bronaber developed to serve the camp, with shops, petrol station etc, known locally as 'Tin-town'. A few buildings remain. After WW2 Plaid Cymru successfully protested against a proposed

expansion of the firing range. The camp closed in 1957 and was used by construction workers at the nuke, then in the 1970's developed as a holiday village, with 200+ chalets.

Porthmadog

Porthmadog ('Port') and Penrhyndeudraeth ('Penrhyn' or 'Penrhyn D')/Minffordd occupy a delicate and strategic position at the mouths of two estuaries. Main roads roar off in all directions, and two Sustrans cycle routes combine to negotiate the bottleneck, with occasional tweaking as improvements are made. The towns are excluded from the National Park. Some cycle runs are included in the companion volume *Llŷn Cycle Guide*, and I would refer you to that volume for details and for a good deal more information about the vicinity. Since publication the by-pass has been completed, providing much needed relief from traffic congestion in Port, though it remains very popular with visitors. Also a cycle path has been completed running alongside the A497 from Porthmadog to Pentrefelin, and on to Cricieth, providing another option for cycle runs to the north and west. In addition I hereby give you two more runs into the hills. The toll bridge over Afon Dwyryd (Pont Briwet) is now toll-free and has been rebuilt in 2014, and provides a link to other routes down towards Harlech.

Route 21 Seven Gates and Seven Veils

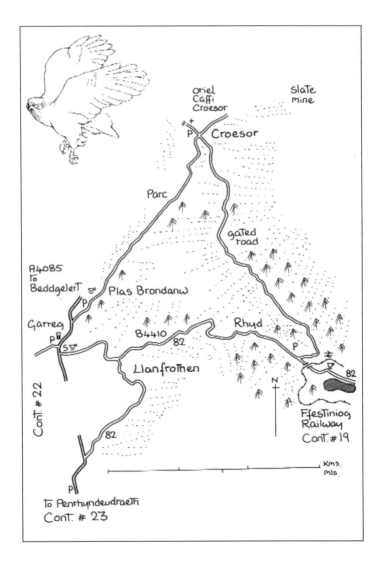

Route 21

Seven Gates and Seven Veils

Run No. 21: *Seven Gates and Seven Veils*
Garreg – Croesor – Tan y Bwlch – Rhyd
Distance: *13k./8ml. (round trip from Llanfrothen)*
Climbs: *150m./500ft. and 100m./330ft.*
Grade: 🚲 🚲 🚲

A straightforward triangular route, you can't go wrong. The road from Tan y Bwlch to Croesor was the pre-Cob mail coach route. Blimey.

The Brondanw Arms was once the ferry terminal for the crossing over to Pren-teg. This is prime Clough Williams-Ellis country, there are plenty of reminders, including the unusual blue paint, culminating in Plas Brondanw. The narrow lane which climbs up to Croesor is quite a bouncy road, verging on 'steep' at times. On your left the big house is Parc, home of the Anwyliaid family, and the name given to one of the most innovative slate workings higher up the valley.

Turn right at Croesor, and the road climbs in earnest, well, earnest is being generous, the road racks up so steeply I was pushing from the bottom of the climb. It is gated too, and a bit like the dance of the seven veils, bits of the view are revealed one by one but we never get the full picture, and the forestry at the top puts an end to the peeking. I have no idea what this road will be like when the trees are being felled, but it would probably be judicious to keep clear on a bike.

From Rhyd the B road engages in a long, steady descent. I am not aware that this is a bikers route, but it wouldn't surprise me.

The minor road forming Route 82 back to Penrhyn is a delight, home to Jay, Cuckoo and Woodpecker.

Cafes at Garreg and Tan y Bwlch (railway station), and a pub in Llanfrothen (Brondanw Arms).

Croesor Quarry

Small scale quarrying began in the 1840s, but even the building of a tramway did little to encourage further development until Moses Kellow became manager in 1895. He electrified the mill, building a hydro-electric power station at the head of the valley, and using Czech motors to drive winches, an electric locomotive, lights, pumps and ventilators. The Kellow pneumatic drill was also a great leap forward. Peak output was 5/6000 tons per year with 300 workers, of whom 70 lived in barracks on the hillside. The quarry closed in 1930 though the power station continued to supply electricity to the grid until the 1950s. Recently it has been

Cnicht from Croesor

revamped at a cost of £1million, and again provides us with electricity.

The mine is linked by an underground passage to the mines above Blaenau.

About 50 years ago the valley was scheduled for drowning as the bottom reservoir of a pumped storage hydroelectric scheme.

Penrhyndeudraeth

Before the Cob was built it had estuaries on both sides and was a traditional fishing and cockling village, the haunt of sailors and smugglers. It was also attractive to those with a little more wealth. Plas Newydd belonged to the Anwyl family, Castell Deudraeth was the estate of David Williams, MP for Meirionnydd, and Portmeirion was made with buildings rescued from all over Europe.

The Narrow Gauge Railways

In the mid C19th three separate narrow-gauge railways reached Port, from Croesor, from Gorseddau and from Blaenau. At first the Ffestiniog railway operated on gravity, with a dandy car on the back of each train carrying a horse, whose duty it was to haul back up the empties. They were replaced by steam in 1863. By then Porthmadog was handling huge quantities of slate, and continued to do so even after the rail transshipment centre at the Minffordd Depot was opened.

Route 22 The Secret Valley

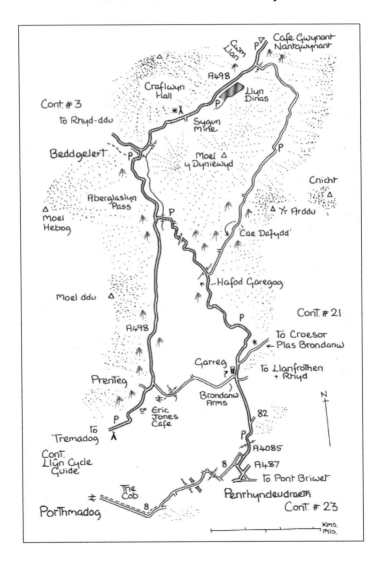

Route 22

The Secret Valley

Run No. 22: *The Secret Valley*
Nanmor
Distance: *26k./16ml. (round trip from Llanfrothen)*
Climb: *200m./660ft.*
Grade: 🚲 🚲

Do this as a loop from Beddgelert, or as a longer run from Porthmadog. Either way it involves main roads in the heart of Snowdonia, and on a weekend in summer, they will be heaving.

The A4085 from Garreg is narrow and twisting in places but virtually flat, running along the valley floor hard pressed against the mountains. At Pont Talyrni the bridge has old carved graffiti including a man with a large eel. Take the road marked Cae Dafydd. Dodging the clutches of twisting oak branches the climb passes the house Cae Dafydd as it gradually lifts you onto a higher plane, a secret oaken paradise opening out to slate spoil heaps and erratics. From the top you look into Cwm Llan with Y Lliwedd on the right and Y Geullt on the left, and the summit of Snowdon bang in the middle.

Plunge down into Nantgwynant. It's a gentle run down to Beddgelert past Llyn Dinas and the Sygun Copper Mine.

The A498 back down to Prenteg and Tremadog is an easy, lovely ride, with, hopefully, not too much traffic.

Pubs and cafes in Beddgelert, also a pub in Llanfrothen (Brondanw Arms), and cafes in Nantgwynant (Cafe Gwynant), Pren-teg (Eric Jones Cafe), and Garreg.

Cwm Llan and Nantgwynant

Beddgelert

The village is known first and foremost for its mid-summer traffic congestion, and secondly for the tale of the faithful hound. This story was first told in 1803 by David Pritchard, landlord of the Royal Goat. At the time it was said to be preferable to sleep with a goat rather than at the Goat. The 'grave' of Gelert has been augmented by Dominic Clares sculptures and Iona McClaggans gates.

A famous resident was Alfred Bestall, creator of Rupert Bear (I could never understand the attraction).

At the beginning of the C20th the plan was for a network of electric railway lines in these valleys, powered by the Cwm Dyli hydro (in Nantgwynant), but the plan never saw fruition, and it wasn't until the 1920s that steam engines operated on what is now called the Welsh Highland Line.

Lôn Gwyrfai has now been extended into Beddgelert (it starts from the car park, past the railway station). It is a relaxed multi-use path partly in the open on tracks but mainly through forest on forest roads, which are rough in places. You are climbing most of the way, and some sections are steep. The scenery is spectacular. It is 7.6 km. up to Rhyd-ddu, and if you choose to descend via the main road it takes about 10 minutes!

Nantgwynant

In the 1950s Nantgwynant was threatened with drowning for a hydro power station.

The Snowdon lakes, Llyn Glaslyn, Llyn Llydaw and Llyn Teyrn all feed the Cwm Dyli Hydro.

Above Pont Bethania, high on Snowdon in Cwm Llan is the Hafod y Llan slate quarry. In the 1860s the owner, Lemon Hart, built an epic tramway down to the valley floor to meet the railway which never came. This is the route of the Watkin Path, built by Sir

Edward Watkin MP and inaugurated in 1892 by Sir William Gladstone.

Above Dinas Emrys the sculptor Dominic Clare has made a giant-sized chair for Owain the Giant. Among the myths associated with the fort is the following. When Vortigern in the C5th fled the Saxon invaders he chose this hill as his retreat and set about building a fort, but each morning the masonry was found collapsed in a heap. Vortigern was advised to seek the help of a young boy born to a virgin mother (bear with me). Eventually one was found, Myrddin Emrys, and brought here, the idea being to sacrifice him to appease the destructive spirit. Hang on, said the boy, who had other ideas for his future, the fort will not stand because of the hidden underground pool containing two dragons, and though the White Dragon of the Saxons has the

Blaen Nanmor

Down to Nantgwynant

upper hand at present, he will soon be defeated by the British Red Dragon. On Vortigerns death the fortress was given to Emrys.

Pren-teg

Pren-teg was once a shipyard and port serving the Pennant valley, when Traeth Mawr was still the sea.

Eric Jones Cafe. Eric was the first Briton to solo up the north wall of the Eiger.

Pont Nanmor

Harlech and Dyffryn Ardudwy

Goodness me, this is a fascinating part of the World. For the cyclist there is work involved, but the rewards are commensurate. The coastal strip, from Llandecwyn on the lower reaches of Afon Dwyryd in the Vale of Ffestiniog, right down to Barmouth at the mouth of Afon Mawddach, is self-contained in that the mountains, the Rhinogs, form a barrier penetrated only by tracks (old drovers routes and one old coaching road).

From north to south the peaks are:

Moel Ysgyfarnogod, 623m/2,056ft

Craig Wion, 566m/1,868ft

Rhinog Fawr, 720m/2,376ft

Rhinog Fach, 712m/2,350ft

Y Llethr, 756m/2,495ft

Diffwys, 750m/2,475ft

These are little known and little visited mountains.

On the plain the linking road is the A496, upon which you will inevitably be cycling at some time. How safe is this road for cyclists? The answer is a big question mark. It is not really busy, but it is narrow in places and twisting and it is hard for motorists to make good progress, which inevitably leads to vehicles trying to squeeze by. Plus, for some unearthly reason, it is also the haunt of motorcycles. Off this road, towards the hills, the minor roads are beautifully quiet, passing through gorgeous landscapes, and are never flat.

A Bit of History

At low tide a 22km causeway known as Sarn Badrig stretches out into Cardigan Bay, acting as a dyke for the green and fertile land of Cantre'r Gwaelod. Seithenyn was partial to a drop of beer, and, unfortunately, being the man in charge of the sluice gate, was responsible for the fatal flood.

During the Ice Age glaciers flowing down the mountains left three such causeways of stony debris reaching into Cardigan Bay, drowned by rising sea levels they resulted in a coastal plain of marsh, peat, salt-marsh clay and even a drowned forest. This was mostly drained in the C18th and C19th, and is partly protected from further inundation by huge sand dunes. It is a regular job in Barmouth, keeping the sand from overrunning the town, and the tidal surge on top of Spring tides in January 2014 demonstrated the vulnerability of this coastal strip.

People moved here in significant numbers around 3,000 years ago, the early and middle Bronze Age, leaving burial mounds, standing stones and stone circles for us to ponder.

In the post-medieval period, estates, large and small, grew to dominate land ownership and land use, changing the landscape significantly at the beginning of the C19th with the common land enclosures of rectilinear fields and a lattice of stone walls and some earthen banks (cloddiau). Unusually for Wales, many outfield barns were built, used to overwinter cattle and to store fodder, reminiscent of the Yorkshire Dales. Beyond the enclosed fields squatters built their 'tŷ unnos'.

In the C19th the railway and the A496 followed the old coastal route, and virtually all the villages were built on these two axis, most of them swollen by a distinct pattern of holiday accommodation, from private villa to seaside holiday chalet, retirement bungalow and, more recently, acres of caravans.

Harlech

The castle was designed by James of St George for King Edward the First. Completed in 1283 the construction involved 1,000 men. Following a siege the castle surrendered to Owain Glyndŵr in 1404 and became his home and military HQ. Four years later it was retaken by the English, his wife and children whipped off to the Tower of London and Glyndŵr vanished.

By the mid C16th Harlech and Dolgellau vied to be top dog in the region, and whilst the gentry wrangled, the poor eeked out a living on the marsh or in the mountains. By the early 1900s Harlech was described as 'the most forlorn, beggarly place imaginable', but the railway brought in the middle classes, and a superior golf course and annual music festival followed. The press of visitors today comes as a horrible shock to cyclists fresh from the hills.

A hundred years ago George Davidson moved into Plas Wernfawr (now part of Coleg Harlech). He was linked with social reformers and anarchists, indeed, Socialist Summer Schools were regularly held in Llanbedr. An impressionistic photographer Davidson co-founded the Linked Ring Brotherhood (representing the Masonic beliefs of 'Good, True and Beautiful') of British artists, which included the Whitby photographer Frank Sutcliffe, though George himself was a millionaire, the managing director of Kodak UK.

Salem Chapel, Pentre Gwynfryn, Llanbedr
An unspoiled C18th chapel with box pews, it features in the painting 'Salem' by S C Vosper, the original hanging in the Lever Art Gallery, Port Sunlight.

RAF Llanbedr
Home of Spitfires, the airfield was used to guard convoys in the Irish Sea, and later for bombing training. There are plans to fly in aircraft as big as Boeing 747s for scrapping, taking the spare parts out by road, and also for the testing and development of drones.

Eisingrug
Glyn Cywarch was the C17th seat of the Ormsby Gores and is now owned by Lord Harlech. Maes-y-neuadd is now a country house hotel.

Talybont (– *head of the bridge*)

Cors y Gedol Hall, built in 1576, was the home of the Griffith Vaughans (and later Mostyns) and is set among woodland and formal gardens.

Bryn Bwbach, Llandecwyn

St Tecwyn's is maintained by a trust affiliated to the Small Pilgrim Places network as a place of private prayer.

Talsarnau.

The 'Ship Aground Inn' was named for the retirement home of Captain John Jones, an C18th naval officer.

Ynys

The church has the graves of many a sea captain.

Tŷ Gwyn y Gamlas (– *the White House on the Canal*) is a three storey warehouse which once acted as a port for Harlech.

Llanfair

Industrial ventures in the area were mostly small scale quarries and metal mines. Llanfair was an underground quarry opening in the 1860s, and then used as an explosive store in the War. It is open as a visitor attraction.

Shell Island

A private holiday complex which occupies a fine location. Day visitors are welcome (£5 per car – cycles go free, I think). Camping, Shop, Restaurant, Bar, an impressive array of 'No' signs.

Route 23 GOC 1 Harlech and Cwm Bychan

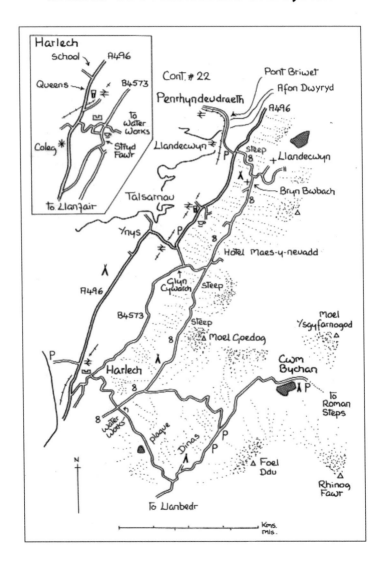

Harlech (inset)
School
A496
Queens
B4573
To Water Works
Coleg
Stryd Fawr
To Llanfair

Cont. # 22
Pont Briwet
Afon Dwyryd
Penrhyndeudraeth
A496
Llandecwyn
P
Steep
8
Llandecwyn
Bryn Bwbach
8
Talsarnau
Ynys
P
8
Hotel Maes-y-nevadd
A496
Glyn Cywarch
Steep
B4573
Steep
8
Moel Goedog
Moel Ysgyfarnogod
P
Harlech
8
Cwm Bychan
P
To Roman Steps
8
Water Works
plaque
Dinas
P
P
Foel Ddu
Rhinog Fawr
To Llanbedr

N

Kms.
mls.

170

Route 23

GOC 1 Harlech and Cwm Bychan

Run No. 23: *GOC 1 Harlech and Cwm Bychan*
Distance: *32k./19½ml.*
Climb: *280m./840ft.*
Grade: 🚲 🚲 🚲

In Yorkshire we do like to bang on about Gods Own Country, but in truth our golden acres are thinly spread, but here the gorgeous land from beach to mountain top is packed into a few square miles. Small, but perfectly formed, as Atholl used to say. These two loops take you from the coast to the heart of the mountains, and back.

Beginning in Harlech, take the old road north, picking up the full traffic only for the flat run from Glan y Wern through Talsarnau to Cilfor, more commonly known as Llandecwyn. Here pick up Sustrans Route 8. It's a steep climb from the off, and, on the tiny roads through oak woodland right through to Eisingrug you could be walking as much as riding. 'Once again it's good to walk' says Annie, claiming to be more observant when she is pushing (she's a natural half-fuller).

From Eisingrug the road steepens (yes, you read that correctly!) into a long climb up towards Moel Goedog (279m/921ft.), but gradually the world opens up to stunning views as the last of the gnarled oaks and high farms are left behind. As often as not you'll find red kite up here. Turn left at the unmarked junction just over the top. forsaking No 8, on to an unlikely looking 'road', narrow but metalled. With cotton grass on either side, this gated road hairpins down vertiginously. Left again to gently ascend through rock and birch, among grey wagtail, nuthatch and mewing buzzards, this magical valley leads to Cwm Bychan. A valley in which to pleasantly while away an afternoon.

For the return, pick up the Harlech road after Dinas and put in a slow, steady, continuous climb to the Cwm Bychan Water Treatment Works, cross No 8, and plunge down in to the chimney pots and turrets of Harlech.

NB The plaque reads:

Tyddyn y Felin
Home of the Poet
John Evans
Author of the work (words)
'The Flowers by the Door'
1892–1949

Pubs and cafes in Harlech, and the pub in Talsarnau (Ship Aground).

above Harlech

Harlech

Llyn Cwm Bychan

Cwm Bychan

Route 24 GOC 2 Harlech and Cwm Nantcol

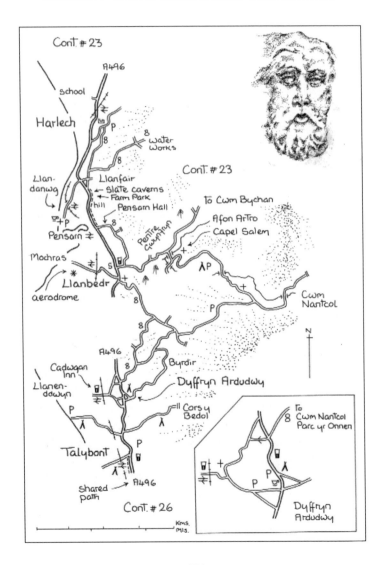

Route 24

GOC 2 Harlech and Cwm Nantcol

Run No. 24: *GOC 2 Harlech and Cwm Nantcol*
Distance: *28k./17½ml.*
Climbs: *250m./825ft. and 140m./460ft.*
Grade: 🚲 🚲 🚲

Beginning in Harlech, take the minor road to Llanfair ('8 Harlech'), then the cycle path alongside the A496 past the Slate Caverns, and the loop past Pensarn Hall to Llanbedr. The valley road through Pentre Gwynfryn, past Capel Salem, past Rhaeadr Nantcol (waterfalls) to Nantcol is a quiet, narrow road, rising and falling (but nothing too serious) through a marvellously invigorating land of woods, walls and slate farms, twisting hazel, colourful rowan and countless oak, with, at the T-junction, the upland valley laid out before you, backed by Rhinog Fawr. Climb to the right on a gated (3) road to Gelli-bant and a magnificent view.

Over the top the land is more open and windswept with isolated barns and monstrous stone walls. Follow the road to Dyffryn Ardudwy but don't miss the sharp turn to the left, through a gate marked 'Byrdir'. This is the road less travelled, with a top dressing of sheep dung and a horseshoe gate fastener. After the isolation of the hills Dyffryn Ardudwy feels like a metropolis.

Whether you tarry or not at the beaches, the way out is on No 8, a climb once more on another enchanting gated road past walling made into an art form, back to Llanbedr. Opposite is the dead-end road and tidal causeway to Mochras (*Shell Island*) past the airfield.

Return the way you came to Harlech, with a detour if you like to see the church being buried by sand at Llandanwg, where there is also a cafe. There are also pubs and cafes in Harlech, Llanbedr, Dyffryn Ardudwy, and Talybont.

Tal-y-bont to Barmouth
Sustrans Route 8 from Tal y Bont to Barmouth runs alongside the A496 on a shared path.

Harlech

Barn, Cwm Nantcol

near Llanbedr

Coed y Brenin

It is big (21,700 acres), and it's a working forest. For all the glamour of the massive Douglas Firs down the bottom end, up at the top it is densely packed Sitka Spruce. Purchased from the Nannau estate in 1922, and planted up to provide 'poles, planks and pit props', it was renamed Coed y Brenin (*the King's Forest*) in 1935 to commemorate the Silver Jubilee of George the Fifth. If you are lucky you'll see polecat, red squirrel, pine marten, goshawk or black grouse; the odd grey squirrel is much more likely.

As a mountain bike centre Coed y Brenin was one of the first in wales, and as its popularity grows so do the facilities. The Visitor Centre incorporates a cafe, bike shop and shop, and the routes include False Teeth, Minotaur, the Beast of Brenin and Cyflym Coch/the Red Fox. Even the car park bristles with adrenaline.

Route 25 A Run Entirely Devoid of Flat

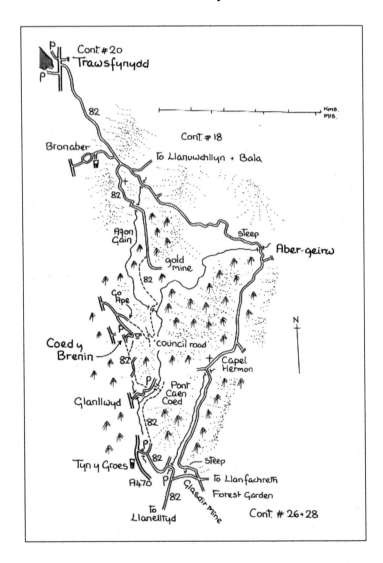

Route 25

A Run Entirely Devoid of Flat

Run No. 25: *A Run Entirely Devoid of Flat*
Coed y Brenin- Abergeirw
Distance: *26k./16ml.*
Climbs: *130m./430ft.; 170m./560ft.; 85m./280ft.; and*
100m./330ft.
Grade: 🚲 🚲 🚲 🚲 🚲

This is quite an adventurous route. It takes you to the back of beyond, but trust me, it works, though one of the uphill stretches is a long drag through working forest, and the one after that is particularly steep.

The first third of the run is in Coed y Brenin on forestry tracks. I have ridden these on a touring bike, which was fine except for a few rough bits and on these you proceed with caution.

The middle third is up on t'moor, with big windswept vistas over to Cadair Idris, the Rhinogs and Arenig Fawr.

The last third is an amazingly long descent, beginning in open space and finishing down a long avenue of towering trees in the forest. If this is 'nature's cathedral' this one is Perpendicular.

Make sure you pick the correct route around Glasdir copper mine, for a mistake would be costly in terms of height gained or lost. From here right the way up through the forest you are following Sustrans Route 82 (this was renumbered some time ago from Route 8, and a few 8s still remain, but it is the same route). MTB routes come and go in a blizzard of signage, and higher up some of the signage is for forestry working, but there is no explanation for the beautiful 'Council Road' signs, in English.

Cafe at Coed y Brenin, pubs at Bronaber (Rhiw Goch Inn) and Tyn y Groes (Tyn y Groes Hotel).

Gwynfynydd

The discovery in 1844 of gold led to the Dolgellau Gold Rush. Pritchard Morgan raised more than a quarter of a ton in 1887, but for others success has been elusive. The recent discovery that gold fell to Earth as gold dust from space, coalescing inside the molten surface because of its weight, and finding its way to the surface again through weathering, adds a little something, don't you think?

Coed y Brenin

Abergeirw

Signs point to Abergeirw as a destination, but, when you're there, blink and you've missed it. The Methodist chapel next to the bridge is a very modest affair.

Dolgellau
'Dol', and known in Liverpool as Dolly-galloo
(– *meadow of monk's cells*)

The county town of Meirionnydd. I have the impression from my first visit in 1969 of a dark, grey, sleepy place (not that I had just dropped in from California!). Not any more, in summer the town throbs with tourists, 'mountaineers' and cyclists. Beginning at the Marian recreation ground and car park is the Mawddach Trail, a 15km/9½ml cycle and walking path with a growing reputation (Best British Bike Path – *The Guardian* March 2012).

The town was a wool town, with leather tanning on the side, specializing in 'webs' or 'Welsh plains', made in water-powered factories in the town. By the 1840s around 1,400 local people were employed in the woolen industry, much of the coarse, thick white cloth being shipped from Barmouth to north America (for use on the covered wagons?)

In Tŷ Meirion (the TIC) is an exhibition devoted to the Meirionnydd Quakers. George Fox toured north Wales in 1657, picking up disciples around Dolgellau and Bala, but they were heavily persecuted and many left for America seeking freedom of worship. Roland Elis of Bryn Mawr, a farm to the south of the town, took the name to his new farm in Pennsylvania. It is supposed that they left behind their hats, being adopted in the C19th as the 'Welsh costume' for women.

Looking forward, Dolgellau clearly has a problem. Roughly 90% of public space in the town centre is given over to motor vehicles, the narrow streets are congested, cyclists and pedestrians lose out and the townscape suffers. Planners could look to the Continent and ban all motor vehicles, apart from deliveries. The by-pass makes this eminently feasible and the town could be transformed. Dream on Horsley.

Dolgellau Cycles, The Old Furnace, Smithfield Street
tel: 01341 423332
email: info@dolgellaucycles.co.uk
www.dolgellaucycles.co.uk
Cycles, spares, accessories for sale. Cycle repairs. Cycle hire, range of cycles, tag-alongs, helmets etc.

Cafe. The popular coffee bar is in the former ironmongers T H Roberts on the site of Owain Glyndŵrs meetings or 'parliament'.

There are other tea shops and pubs too.

Leaving Dolgellau on a Bicycle

The town occupies the valley of Afon Wnion, lapping up the valley on both sides. None but the hardened road cyclist uses the A470, especially going south, for after the improved uphill section to Cross Foxes, you climb either the Bwlch Oerddrws or the Bwlch Llyn Bach (on the A487), not places for the fainthearted. The A494 to Bala is not in the same league of ferocity, but you have to share it with milk tanker, white van, coach and caravan.

Otherwise, going west, the Mawddach Trail is simply sublime; to the north 'Route 82' past Cymer abbey is an easy-peasy run and the minor roads up to Llanfachreth are quiet but involve steady climbing. To the south, the road marked 'Cader Idris' involves a similar head-down steady climb of around 150m./ 500ft., but takes you to a rather marvellous land on the flanks of the mountain. To the east 'Route 8' towards Cross Foxes is a rather brutish climb of 230m./760ft..

For the Sustrans Route Planners travelling south from Dolgellau caused some head scratching. As mentioned above, both passes are out, the A493 coast road is used by road cyclists, but is a narrow, twisting road clinging to the sea cliff, so they opted for 'Ffordd Ddu' (*the Black Road*) for 82, a rough track hacking over to Dyffryn Dysynni, and a track into the Dyfi Forest (8), both of which climb to over 400m./1320ft..

Cymer abbey

Route 26 Llwybr Mawddach Trail

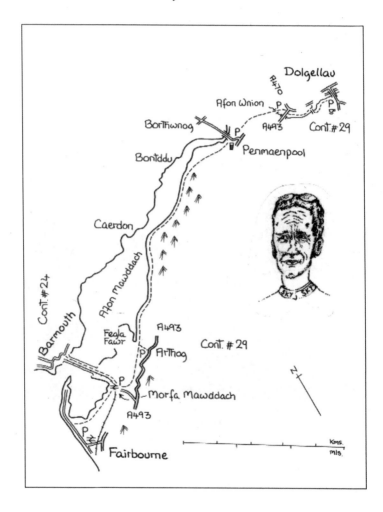

Dolgellau

A470

Afon Wnion

Borthwnog

Bontddu

Caerdon

Penmaenpool

A493

Cont.# 29

P

Afon Mawddach

Cont # 24

Barmouth

Fegla Fawr

A493

P Arthog

Cont. # 29

P

Morfa Mawddach

A493

N

P

Fairbourne

Kms.
Mls.

Route 26

Llwybr Mawddach Trail

Run No. 26: *Llwybr Mawddach/Mawddach Trail*
Dolgellau to Barmouth and Fairbourne
Distance: *15k./9½ml.*
Grade: 🚲

- 9½ miles/15km. from Barmouth to Dolgellau.
- Flat. Well, obviously it rises and falls a bit, but indiscernibly.
- The surface is good, tarmac or hardcore. After heavy rain it can get a bit messy.
- Car parks in Barmouth, Dolgellau, at the new Mawddach bridge, Penmaenpool, Arthog and Morfa Mawddach station.
- Cafes in Dolgellau, Fairbourne and Barmouth.
- Pubs in Dolgellau, Barmouth, Fairbourne and Penmaenpool.
- The trail deserves its recommendation as one of the best, it is packed full of interest.

At the Dolgellau end the Trail begins in the car park near Y Bont Fawr/the Big Bridge. Follow the signs around the Marian recreation ground.

At the Barmouth end, extend the run a little from the viaduct, following the coast around to the end of the promenade (this is Sustrans Route 8).

Also, from Morfa Mawddach, work has recently been completed on the flood embankment, which is now topped with a cycle path, which you can follow into Fairbourne (Y Friog) or to the ferry at the tip of the spit. There is no longer a toll over the viaduct.

Pubs and cafes in Barmouth and Dolgellau. Also the George III Hotel at Penmaenpool, and a cafe at the station in Fairbourne.

Penmaenpool

Pont Borthwnog. The toll bridge was built in 1879 and could be opened for sailing ships. Here were wharves and shipyards.

The GWR signal box is an RSPB observatory.

The pub, the George III, was built around 1650.

Borthwnog

The epicentre of the gold rush, which reached fever pitch when Pritchard Morgan struck a rich vein in 1887. Clogau Mine, above Bontddu, survives with a fine reputation as a supplier of wedding rings for the Princes of Wales.

Further along on the north side is the early Victorian mansion Caerdon Hall, built together with the 'Basque' church, by Rev. Jelf,

Afon Mawddach

and used to entertain such luminaries as Ruskin, Tennyson, Wordsworth and Darwin.

Arthog

The GWR opened the Ruabon-Barmouth railway in 1868, carrying holidaymakers to Barmouth and beyond, and slate the other way. It closed in 1965. The slate mine is now a caravan site.

Arthog Bog is an SSSI (reed bunting etc).

Morfa Mawddach (Barmouth Junction) was a triangular railway junction with the Cambrian Coast line. The viaduct was built in 1867.

Fegla Fawr. The businessman Soloman Andrews began to build a 'family resort' here in the late C19th, but it failed commercially. It was used by the Royal Marines as a training base prior to the D-Day landings.

Fairbourne (Y Friog originally called Ynys Faig)

Construction of the village began in the late 1890s by Mr Arthur McDougall (of the flour) using bricks from his brickworks, conveyed on a horse-drawn tramway, now a narrow-gauge railway. A small ferry crosses over to Barmouth. Arthur McDougall planted a rose in each garden.

Barmouth/Abermaw – 'Bermo'

By the late C18th Barmouth was a vital port in the export of wool, many of the ships being locally built, and in 1892 it had its own shipping line, the Aberdyfi and Barmouth Steamship Co., with regular runs to Liverpool. The railway brought a decline in the port, but an increasing number of tourists, among them Romantics and Academics. Ruskin formed the Guild of St George,

Llwybr Llyn – Traws – Lake Path

a social housing experiment in the town, on land owned by Mrs Talbot, who also gave the National Trust their first property in 1895, Dinas Oleu/Castle of Light.

As well as the amusements, Barmouth boasts the Music Festival in July, the Arts Festival in September, the start of the Three Peaks race, and the best dentists in Gwynedd.

Route 27 Nannau and the Great Stone Arch

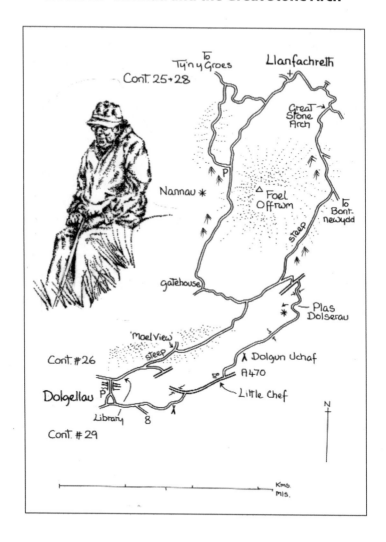

To Ty'n y Groes
Cont. 25 + 28
Llanfachreth
Great Stone Arch
P
Nannau *
△ Foel Offrwm
To Bont-newydd
steep
gatehouse
Plas Dolserau
Moel View
steep
Cont. #26
Dolgun Uchaf
A470
Little Chef
Dolgellau
P
Library 8
Cont. #29
N

Kms.
Mls.

Route 27

Nannau and the Great Stone Arch

Run No. 27: *Nannau and the Great Stone Arch*
Distance: *17k./11ml.*
Climb: *220m./725ft.*
Grade: 🚲 🚲

The first of two runs described around the Hill of Sacrifice, but these lanes can be ridden any number of ways.

The steepest bit of the ascent to Nannau is at the bottom, out of Dolgellau, but you are climbing most of the way. This is gorgeous estate country. There is a descent from the Precipice Walk car park to Llanfachreth of 80m./260ft. Pass under the Arch. In a mile the left fork takes you to Bontnewydd and Brithdir via the B4416 (Run no. 28), the right fork steeply descends to the Bala road, which you cross and pass Plas Dolserau (Holiday Fellowship) and Dolgun Uchaf (The old Quaker meeting room). Emerge on to the A470 at the Little Chef, and drop back down into town.

Pubs and cafes in Dolgellau.

Llanfachreth and the Hill of Sacrifice

The Mawddach Trail is flat. No gear changing is required. The low hills between the valleys of the rivers Mawddach and Wnion are anything but, with plenty of climbing on adventurous, twisting, looping lanes through a delightfully varied land of woods and pasture with hills and cottages folded into the hillside. The views across to Cadair are spectacular.

The dominant hill is Moel Offrwm, *the Hill of Sacrifice*, from which the ancients used to hurl prisoners to their deaths. The main approach is through Porth yr Euog, the Gateway of the Guilty.

The local potentates were the Nanneys and Vaughans of Hengwrt and Nannau. One of the ancestors, Meurig ab Ynyr Fychan, lies, in effigy in the Church of St Mary in Dolgellau. Llanfachreth was the estate village for the Nannau estate, which dates back to Cadwgan ap Bleddyn ap Cynfyn, Prince of Powys, in the C12th. The house has been rebuilt five times since then, the last (or latest) being 1788–96 by 'Yr Hen Syr Robert', Robert Vaughan, who also built many of the roads, walls and houses nearby and in the town, partly to relieve unemployment after the Napoleonic Wars, including Y Garreg Fawr, the Great Stone Arch. Many of the cottages have curving slate roofs, and some were built with porches on rounded pillars. The estate contained a deer park and ancient woodland, of which the mighty oaks are a remnant.

After the first World War Nannau became a convalescent home for shell-shocked veterans, and during the second World War it sheltered a girls school from Kent. The estate began to break up soon after, and the house sold in 1996. Since then it has been an hotel, country club, time-share complex and caravan site. Dry rot has ravaged the house, which is just a shell.

Route 28 The Meeting of the Waters

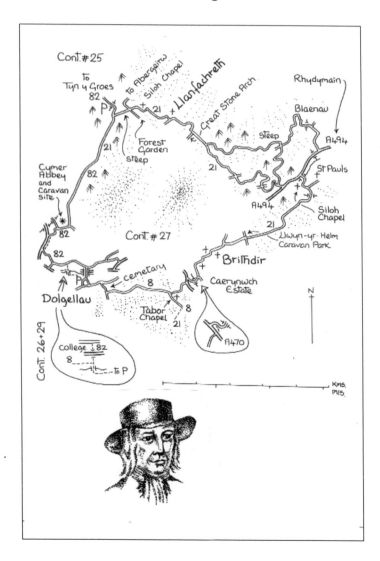

198

Route 28

The Meeting of the Waters

Run No. 28: *The Meeting of the Waters*
Dolgellau – Cymer – Llanfachreth – Brithdir –
Dolgellau
Distance: *29k./18ml.*
Climbs: *2220m./725ft.; 185m./610ft.; and 100m./330ft.*
Grade: 🚲 🚲 🚲

From Dolgellau follow the blue 82 signs towards Llanelltyd, past Cymer abbey on to the single track road above the mighty Mawddach. As Afon Wen joins the Mawddach, leave 82 and follow the signs for Llanfachreth. This road is very steep. Past Siloh Chapel and left in the village towards Rhyd-y-main. Do not pass under the Arch but begin the long, looping descent down to Pont Llanrhaeadr over Afon Wnion. If you feel like an extra climb for extra views, take the road up to Ystum-gwadnaeth. This deposits you at a crossroads with three gates, the lanes all looking equally unpromising, among the possessions of an avid collector of rusty machinery. You cannot go wrong, all three lanes lead to the Bala road.

Cross Pont Llanrhaeadr to Bryncoedifor, and another Siloh Chapel, and climb again, crossing Afonnau Celynog and Helygog to Brithdir. This is a beautiful part of the World, all tinkling streams, birdsong and ancient woodland. Left on the B4416 to Pont ar Ddibyn over Afon Clywedog, over the A470 and up to Tabor Chapel. The descent to Dolgellau is mighty.

Pubs and cafes in Dolgellau, and the Cross Foxes.

Llanelltyd
Cymer Abbey
A few ruins remain of this Cistercian Abbey, founded in 1199, and taking its name from 'Kymer deu Dyfyr', the *Meeting of the Waters*.

The church of St Illtyd is a simple C16th one with a Norman font.

The old bridge is C15th. Buildings nearby used to be warehouses for the export of wool, carried on ships built at the adjoining Maes y Garnedd yard. Ten ships were built in the estuary yards annually, mostly sloops and brigs, but some schooners too.

Brithdir
The church of St Mark was built on the bequest of the Rev. Charles Tooth, chaplain of St Marks church in Florence, and built in the north Italian country style, in 1896, with beaten copper panels, choir stalls in Spanish walnut and decorative lead work.

Tabor
A Quaker meeting house. Used since 1847 by the Congregationalists.

Route 29 Cadair Idris/Islaw'r-dref

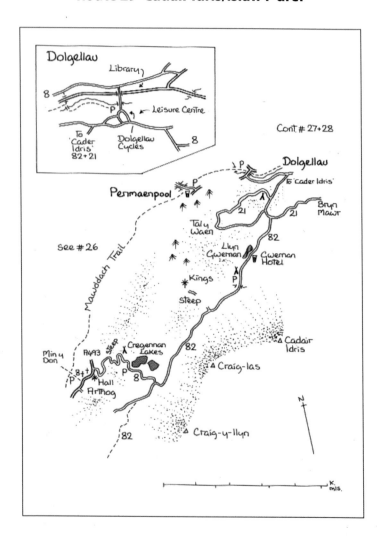

Route 29

Cadair Idris/Islaw'r-dref

Run No. 29: *Cadair Idris/Islaw'r-dref*
Distance: *24k./15ml.*
Climb: *205m./675ft.*
Grade: 🚲 🚲 🚲

Route 21. This is the place to tell you about Route 21. The waymarking is good and clear and marked anticlockwise only. The run includes a couple of sections which are rough, rough enough for gingerly progress only on my touring bike.

It begins in Dolgellau, up the road marked 'Cader Idris', looping around Tal y Waen before setting off across the face of Cadair. On this loop you'll come across some strange rusting machinery, which was used to raise and lower targets on the Penmaenucha military shooting range. This range has its origins in the Boer War, but the remnants are from the first World War. There is plenty of up and down as you cross streams pouring down the mountainside. At Afon Aran Route 21 climbs again, still on metalled roads, but viciously, followed by two miles of track, at first through forestry, emerging at the Tabor Chapel. Up again to Cross Foxes and down the Caerynwch estate road. The track cutting the corner to Brithdir is open fell in the middle. Thereafter it follows my Run No 28, but in reverse.

Given the choice, I prefer the following run out of Dolgellau.

Islaw'r-dref (which translates roughly as the township in the lower ground)

Cadair Idris from Llynnau Cregennen

Take the road out of Dolgellau marked 'Cader Idris' and climb 160m./540ft.. It is a steady heads-down climb with a couple of steeper bits. You enter a lovely timeless land of high pasture and walls, with a feeling of undisturbed calm. Cadair Idris has its head in the clouds to the south. There is a further pull out to the valley head, but you've done most of the climbing already. The ice-sliced hill is Craig-las. I've written only one word in my notes for Llynnau Cregennan, but I've written it twice... gorgeous. The cracking descent is switchbacked, steep and gated. Drop behind Arthog Hall to the A493, turn left through the village for a mile. The track marked Min y Don takes you to the Mawddach trail and hence back to Dolgellau.

Pubs and cafes in Dolgellau, also the Gwernan Hotel and the George III in Penmaenpool.

near Dolgellau

Near Gellilydan

Tywyn

The guide book for the 'Sunshine Coast of Mid Wales' describes Tywyn as 'a good safe sea-bathing place and holiday resort'. We used to come here on holiday when I were a lad. Dad came to climb mountains, Mum to sit on the beach and chat, I came for the steam engines and my sister because she had no choice. The HF centre is for sale. Tywyn is popular with Brummies, a caravan, chalet and retirement town.

But it has a history.

St Cadfans Church was the southern equivalent of Clynnog Fawr, a gathering place for pilgrims on the way to Enlli/Bardsey. See the *Llŷn Cycle Guide* for details. The main nave and side isles are original, Norman, C11th. The rest has been rebuilt. It holds the early C8th Cadfan Stone, a C13th Sanctus Bell and C14th effigies of the Crying Knight and the Unnamed Priest. A little further north the churches at Llanegryn (St Mary and Egryn) and Llangelynnin (St Celynnin) are both simple churches worth a visit.

Cycle Routes out of Town

I am describing two runs from Tywyn, for the mountains press heavily on the coast here, and choice is not abundant, plus this is the very south-western corner of Snowdonia.

Route 30 Lôn Dysynni

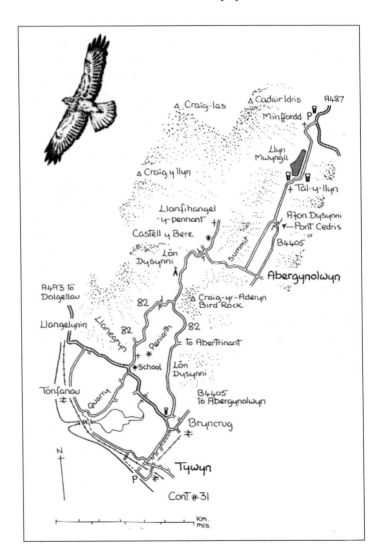

Craig-las

Cadair Idris

A487

Minffordd P

Llyn Mwyngil

Craig y llyn

Tal-y-llyn

Llanfihangel -y-pennant

Afon Dysynni
Pont Cedris

Castell y Bere

B4405

Lôn Dysynni

Summit

Abergynolwyn

A493 To Dolgellau

Craig-yr-Aderyn Bird Rock

82

Llangelynin

Llanegryn

82

82

Peniarth

To Abertrinant

School

Lôn Dysynni

Tonfanau

Quarry

B4405 To Abergynolwyn

Bryncrug

N

Tywyn

P

Cont #31

Km.
mls.

Lôn Dysynni

Run No. 30: *Lôn Dysynni*
Distance: *48k./30½ml. (Minffordd to Tywyn and return)*
Climb: *60m/200ft.*
Grade: 🚲

First a little geography. Afon Dysynni drains Cadair Idris and other mountains, and flows down a classic U-shaped valley, scoured out by an ice glacier. During warmer periods in the Ice Ages, melting caused the glacier to drop the rock contained within in heaps called moraines. The valley contains two of these. The first blocked the main valley west of Abergynolwyn, forcing the river to cut through the ridge into Dyffryn Dysynni; the second blocked drainage enough to form the lake at Tal-y-llyn, Llyn Mwyngil.

For the cyclist exploring these two valleys the arrival of the seemingly innocuous B4405 is not to be taken lightly, for this is one of the service roads to Tywyn, and can be very busy at times.

Lôn Dysynni is a laid back cycleway, like a Thelonius Monk track, sit back, chill and enjoy. At regular intervals there are benches, with bike-shaped bike stands. The cycling is effortless, the countryside lush and calm. I have reproduced the cycleway on the map, and added two extensions. Along the B4405 up to Tal-y-llyn and the Cadair Idris car park at Minffordd, and, at the other end, the building of Pont Tonfannau now gives the option of an additional laid-back extension. I met the bridge painters who said painting Pont Tonfannau is like painting the Forth Bridge, only tougher.

Pubs and cafes in Tywyn. Cafes and a pub (Railway Inn) in Abergynolwyn, and pubs at Tal-y-llyn (Pen-y-bont Hotel and the Ty'n y cornel Hotel) and Minffordd (Minffordd Hotel).

Ysgol Craig y Deryn
Controversially four village schools were closed for this £5.4 million new primary school near Llanegryn. It is a state of the art building with photovoltaics, rainwater recycling and a biomass boiler.

Castell y Bere
A ruined castle on a narrow rock spur, the last of Llywelyn Fawr's strongholds to fall to Edward Longshanks.

Llanfihangel-y-Pennant. The C16th church has a leper window, but the village is best known for Mary Jones, a weavers daughter, who walked to Bala at the age of 16, a 50 mile round trip, partly barefoot to save wear on her boots, across rough country, to buy a bible from Thomas Charles in 1800.

Dysynni Valley
The valley was drained from the late 1700s by the Corbets of Ynysmaengwyn to create flat, fertile land. The drainage these days is controlled by sluice gates, which could be a problem when sea levels rise. The tidal surges in early 2014 certainly damaged the railway here, and in other places along this coastal strip.

Bird Rock/Craig yr Aderyn
Nesting site for chough and cormorant among other sea birds.

Cycle Hire. Bird Rock Cycle Hire, Cefncoch, Bryncrug.
tel: 01654 712193

pat @cefn-coch.co.uk
www.cefn-coch.co.uk

Peniarth

The estate and its caravan site occupy a central site in Dyffryn Dysynni, and runs to approx. 14,000 acres, including Cadair Idris. It was reputedly won in a game of chance with King Henry the Fifth in 1412, the estate and most of Merionethshire too. In 2006 Lord of the Manor William Williams-Wynne came close to losing it in a divorce settlement with his wife Roo. Mr Williams-Wynne said 'The whole thing sucks'.

Minffordd (Tal-y-llyn)

At Dolau Cae lived Howell Idris MP, the founder of Idris fizzy drinks.

Bird Rock/Craig yr Aderyn

Route 31 Cwm Maethlon/Happy Valley

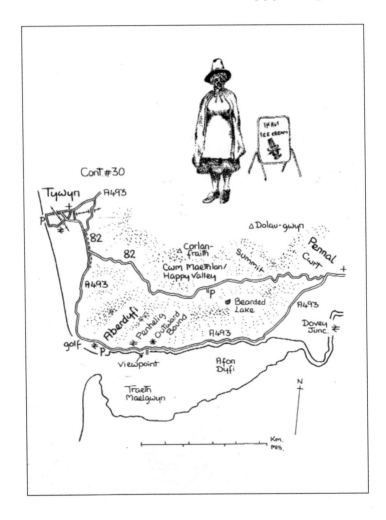

Cont. #30

Tywyn A493

P

82

82

A493

Corlan-fraith

Cwm Maethlon/Happy Valley

Summit

Dolau-gwyn

Pennal Cwrt

P

Bearded Lake

A493

Aberdyfi

Panhelig

Outward Bound

A493

Dovey Junc.

golf P

Viewpoint

Afon Dyfi

Traeth Maelgwyn

N

Km.
mis.

Route 31

Cwm Maethlon/Happy Valley

Run No. 31: *Cwm Maethlon/Happy Valley*
Distance: *29k./18ml.*
Climb: *200m./590ft.*
Grade: 🚲 🚲

In my mind 'Happy Valley' equates with wet caravan holidays so I prefer the Welsh, which translates roughly as the bountiful valley.

This is a straightforward loop from Tywyn. The A493 has a shared path to the Cwm Maethlon turn off (and beyond). At the other end, in Cwrt, turn right and return on the A493 via Aberdyfi. You can see the problem. Everything depends on the traffic on the A493. This road is well used by cyclists, and not just the road chaps, unsurprisingly for this is a cracking run with the whole estuary laid out at your wheels. Pity about the traffic, but it is a slow road anyway so you don't feel too much pressure on a bike. Remember to ride positively and make vehicles overtake (sorry if the record is stuck). Remember also that the average time in which a driver loses patience and then does something silly is between 5 and 10 seconds. There are few places at which you can actually stop and pull off the road safely, but the stand out one is just to the west of the Outward Bound centre. A footbridge over the railway takes you to benches with a full panorama. Last time I was there I watched an osprey hunting over the estuary, and rising smoke opposite from a charcoal burn.

Cwm Maethlon is an easy, quiet ride with a pull up to the summit, accompanied by wren and woodpecker, wagtail and stonechat. There are clefts and folds to linger over, reminiscent of the Lake District without the multitudinous hordes.

The drop on the east side is 170m./550ft. in a mile.

Pubs and cafes in Tywyn and Aberdyfi.

Llyn Barfog/The Bearded Lake
It is high above you in the hills, and was home to the monster Afanc, until he or she was killed by King Arthur.

Pennal
The church has a copy of the Pennal Policy from 1406, in which Owain Glyndŵr sets out his conditions for recognizing the Pope of Avignon and not the Pope of Rome (of all the things he had to worry about...).

The road from here to Cwrt is Wtra'r Beddau, the Lane of Graves, said to have been first paved with the gravestones of Welshmen and Yorkists under Harri ap Gwilym, all killed in a Wars of the Roses battle.

Aberdyfi
A successful port and shipbuilding centre until the arrival of the railway. Now a successful, and busy, sailing and holiday centre. The Outward Bound here was the first one, established in 1941. The local rowing club uses 4-oared Celtic longboats, and the Golf Club was the first in Wales.

Marconi
On your way back into Tywyn you pass the Marconi Bungalows, built to house workers at the Long Wave Receiver, working in duplex with the transmitter at Waunfawr. You may ask why Marconi did not use Ireland instead, it being that bit closer to America, and the answer is, he did, but between 1916 and 1922 Ireland was experiencing the last civil war to take place on British

soil (though republicans argue that the 'Troubles' in the north were also a civil war).

Dyfi Junction/Cyffordd Dyfi
The railway junction is close to the meeting place of Gwynedd, Powys and Ceredigion in Dyfed (part of the original realm of Y Deheubarth). Here was a convenient meeting place for leaders from the three Kingdoms. Here the Treaty of Aberdyfi agreed that Llywelyn Fawr be leader of the Welsh Lords, and to here also came the European ambassadors for the first meeting of Owain Glyndŵrs Parliament in Machynlleth, to meet the new 'Prince of the Nation'.

Today a new European signaling system is being installed to enable faster, more frequent trains to run on the single line to Welshpool.

Machynlleth – 'Mach'

A small town in Dyffryn Dyfi/Dovey Valley, Machynlleth sits outside the National Park, and is actually in Powys. The Lonely Planet Guide says that Mach 'punches well above its weight', and is 'saturated in historical significance'. It talks of 'eco-magneticism' and 'mountain biking'. For the long-distance cyclist Sustrans Route 8 passes through the town, forking both north and south of Mach.

Four dates are especially significant:

- 1291. A Royal Charter was given to the Lord of Powys with the right to hold a market every wednesday, and two fairs a year (these would have been hiring fairs).

- 1404. Owain Glyndŵr sited his Parliament here, and was crowned Prince of Wales near Parliament House in Maen Gwyn Street. The singlemindedness of the locals is further indicated by the side streets named Garrison (Gariswn) Street and Barracks, a reminder that Parliamentary troops were kept here in the mid C17th to keep order.

- 1874. To celebrate the 21st birthday of their eldest son, Viscount Castlereagh, his parents, Mary Cornelia and Viscount Seaham (later Lord Vane and then the Marquess of Londonderry) organized the collection of a subscription from the townspeople to build a clock tower. They lived in Plas Machynlleth, which became the Council Offices, then the Celtica Heritage Centre and from 2006 it has been run by the Town Council as a restaurant and for community benefit.

- 1973. The Centre for Alternative Technology opened up the road. Despite some ups and downs it is still going strong, with an emphasis these days on sustainable living and education. The local renewable energy industries are a useful spin-off.

The Dyfi Bridge has obviously been important to the town, the first one being built in the C16th. The complimentary cycle path bridge is more recent.

Mention could also be given to the fine church gates, erected in 1843 at a cost of £4 and a pig.

Route 32 Fifty Shades of Green

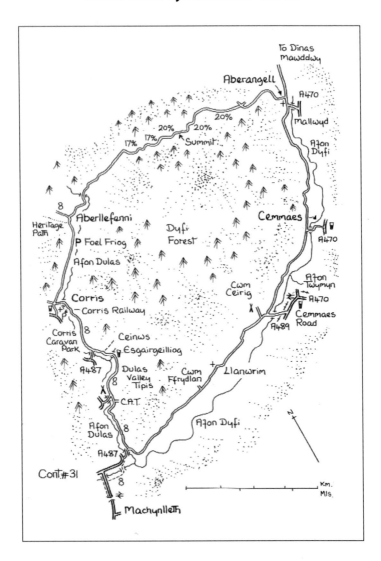

Route 32

Fifty Shades of Green

Run No. 32:   *Fifty Shades of Green*
                Corris – Aberangell – Machynlleth
Distance: 38k./24ml.
Climb: 330m./1090ft.
Grade: 🚲 🚲 🚲 🚲

A simple loop, but one encompassing many different hues, and you'll be unlucky if you encounter more than half a dozen vehicles all day.

Corris is an ex-mining village shoehorned into the bottom of the valley of Afon Dulas. Follow the valley up through Aberllefenni. It's a bit like riding through the stage set of a Wagnerian opera, and though Robert Plant and Jimmy Page once played a gig up at the quarry, neither had pigtails and a horned helmet, as far as I know.

With little warning the road rears up. Oak and birch stay with you for a while, to provide encouragement, but soon you are in no-nonsense, no-compromise forest. I am still prejudiced against spruce forest having spent so much time in dark Scottish ones, infested with midge and tick. I even managed to pick up ticks while cycling. The smell of pine greets you, then it is quiet, with the forest birds hanging about up in the canopy. Two more kicks of 17% and 20% then its steady graft to the summit and the reward of a glimpse of Cadair Idris. A total climb of 330m./1,090ft.. The descent is in two long drops of 20% and then you're back in civilization, with the remnants of a beech avenue.

Turn left for refreshments at Minllyn, Mallwyd or Dinas

Mawddwy. Otherwise turn right and you are on delightful back roads on the valley edge with the remnants of a railway beneath you and the graceful, meandering river. All the traffic is on the opposite side of the valley. This is Powys, and slightly different, brick, half-timbered houses, thick oaks and a softer, greener valley. Less drama and more subtlety, like the fish course before the beef (or for vegans the green lentils before the chick peas).

The valley widens as it collects tributaries. Machynlleth is tucked away behind a hill. As you cross back into Gwynedd take a right up into the Dulas valley for a somewhat uneven ride back to Corris, passing the C.A.T. and various Tipi projects.

Having lived in Scotland you'd think I would be used to the military (we once had a tank come down the drive, he was lost), but I'll never get used to the low-flying jets.

Pubs and cafes in Machynlleth. There is a cafe and pub in Minllyn (Buckley Arms), and other pubs in Corris (Slaters Arms), Ceinws (Tafarn Dwynant), Mallwyd (Brigands), Dinas Mawddwy (Red Lion), Cemmaes (Penrhos Arms), and Cemmaes Road (Dovey Valley Hotel). C.A.T. has a cafe.

Aberllefenni
The slate mines closed in 2003, operated for the last 50 years by Gwilym and Dewi Lloyd as Wincilate. The mill continues working, processing slate from Blaenau and Penrhyn, though it is transported by lorry rather than the Corris railway.

Lord Buckley
A Lancashire businessman, he bought the Buckley estate, over 10,000 acres, and built a railway in the valley of Afon Dyfi. Plas Dinas was built in 1872, but destroyed by fire in 1917.

Dyfi Valley

The valley is a UNESCO biosphere, one of only two in Britain, an area in which people work to balance the conservation of biodiversity with its sustainable use.

Glantwymyn/Cemais

The unusual house with central chimneys is Cemais Bychan/Tan y ffordd, built as a timber framed mansion in 1632 by Lewis Anwyl. It was taken over in 1920 by the Local Authority and split into two to provide small-holdings for men returning from the war.

The Dyfi Forest/Coed Dyfi

The forest was planted between the wars with the centre of operations the Dyfi Instructional Centre at Ceinws/ Esgaingeilliog, with offices, 14 houses, a church, village hall, library and garage. The 'camp' is largely empty now, and active consideration is being given to its future.

Mountain Biking

Machynlleth is becoming a MTB centre, with the Nant yr Arian trail centre south of the town. In the Dyfi Forest Cli-machX, a 15km. ride begins in Ceinws.

Reditreks Hostel, Heol Powys, Machynlleth, is the home of J.P.'s Bike Salon, repairs and spares.

Wheelism, based in Dinas Mawddwy offers bike coaching, training and courses.

Corris Tramway

The tramway delivered slate from Corris and above down to the river port of Derwen-las, and then to the railway when it arrived in 1862.

Bron yr Aur

The Rev. John Dale, the present owner, has appealed to worshippers to be left alone please, for the cottage was where Stairway to Heaven was conceived.

Dinas Mawddwy and Mallwyd

A sheep and lead mining and slate area, but the Brigands Inn is a reminder of the days when the criminal fraternity, ousted from Ysbyty Ifan, came down here en masse. Judge Lewis Owen sentenced many of them to death upon capture, though he himself was killed by outlaws.

Minllyn

In the old quarry sheds is Y Gymdeithas Wlân, a weavers co-operative, before becoming the Meirion Mill Woollen Centre. It has a coffee shop.

I would like to acknowledge my debt to the three books written by Alun John Richards and illustrated with fine photographs by Jean Napier:
  – *A Tale of Two Rivers; Mawddach and Dyfi.*
  – *Two Snowdonia Rivers; Glaslyn and Dwyryd.*
  – *The River Conwy; Source to Sea.*
Published by Gwasg Carreg Gwalch.

Cycle Shops, Repair and Hire

Summit Cycles, 31 Heol Maengwyn, Machynlleth.
☎ 01654 700411

Dolgellau Cycles, The Old Furnace, Smithfield St., Dolgellau.
Cycle hire, repair and sales.
☎ 01341 423332
www.dolgellaucycles.co.uk
email: info@dolgellaucycles.co.uk

Bird Rock Cycle Hire, Cefn Coch, Bryncrug, Tywyn.
☎ 01654 712193
www.cefn-coch.co.uk
email: pat@cefn-coch.co.uk

Beics Brenin, Coed y Brenin. Cycle hire, sales, repairs.
☎ 01341 440728
www.beicsbrenin.co.uk

Beddgelert Bikes, Beddgelert. Bike hire,sales and service.
☎ 01766 890434
email: peter@beddgelertbikes.co.uk

K K Cycles, 141 High Street, Porthmadog.
☎ 01766 512310

Beics Betws, Heol y Ficerdy, Betws-y-coed. Cycle hire, sales and service.
☎ 01690 710766

Snowdon Bikefix, Conwy Falls, Betws-y-Coed. Repairs.

Llanberis Bike Hire, 34 High St., Llanberis.
☎ 01286 872787
email: llanberisbikehire@gmail.com

Cycle Tech Snowdonia, High St., Llanberis. Mobile repairs.
☎ 01286 871188
www.theframedbicycleco.com
email: hi@theframedbicycleco.com

Beics Menai, 1 Slate Quay, Caenarfon. Hire, sales and service.
☎ 01286 676804
www.beicsmenai.co.uk

Greens Bike Shop, near Caernarfon, mobile bike servicing.
☎ 01286 871125   ☎ 07587095381
www.greensbikeshop.co.uk
email: post@greensbikeshop.co.uk

Cyclewales.net, Salem Chapel, Talysarn, Pen-y-Groes.
Bike hire, workshop and sales.
☎ 0800 7831489   ☎ 07733 121585
www.cyclewales.net

Evolution Bikes, 141 High St., Bangor.
☎ 01248 355770
www.evolution-bikes.co.uk

West End Cycles, Conway Rd., Llandudno Junction.
☎ 01492 593811
www.westendcycles.com

Halfords, Bangor and Llandudno.

The Bike Van. Mobile repairs and service.
☎ 01286 881175   ☎ 07805 957402
www.thebikevan.co.uk

Budget Accomodation

In addition to the YHA hostels at:
- Kings, Dolgellau
- Bryn Gwynant, Nantgwynant
- Snowdon Ranger
- Llanberis
- Snowdon Pen-y-Pass
- Idwal
- Betws-y-coed
- Ro-wen
- Conwy

there are the following bunkhouses and hostels.

Corris Hostel ☎ 01654 761686
Braich Goch Bunkhouse Inn, Corris ☎ 01654 761229
Toad Hall, Machynlleth ☎ 01654 700597
Cefn Coed, Penmaenpool, Dolgellau ☎ 01341 423584
Torrent Bunk Barn, Dolgun Uchaf, Dolgellau ☎ 01341 422269
Hyb Bunkhouse, Dolgellau ☎ 01341 421755
Bala Backpackers ☎ 01678 521700
Bala Bunk House ☎ 01678 520738
Maentwrog Bunkhouse ☎ 01766 590231
Bunkhouse, Elen's Castle Hotel, Dolwyddelan ☎ 01690 750207
Bryn Tirion Farm Bunkhouse, Dolwyddelan ☎ 01690 750366
Glan Aber Bunkhouse, Glan Aber Hotel, Betws-y-coed
　　☎ 01690 710325
Plascurig Hostel, Capel Curig ☎ 01690 720225
Glan Llugwy Bunkhouse, Capel Curig ☎ 01690 720213
Bryn Tyrch Farm Bunk House, Capel Curig ☎ 01690 720414

plus others around Capel Curig, visit
www.visitcapel.fsnet.co.uk/bunkhouses
Bryn Du Mountain Centre, Llanberis ☎ 01286 870556
Jesse James Bunkhouse, Ysgubor Gwersylla, Llnaberis
☎ 01286 870521
White Peris Lodge, Dinorwig ☎ 01286 870853
Snowdon House Bunkhouse, Nant Peris ☎ 01286 650152
Ogwen Valley Bunkhouse, Bethesda ☎ 01248 601958
Tyddyn Du Bunkhouse, Gerlan, Bethesda ☎ 01248 6600670
Totters Hostel, Plas Porth Yr Aur ☎ 01286 672963
Bunkhouse, Cwt y Coed, Bethel, Caernarfon ☎ 01248 673280
Bunkhouse, Pentre Bach, Waunfawr ☎ 01286 650643
Platts Farm Bunkhouse, Llanfairfechan ☎ 01248 680105
Conwy Valley Backpackers Barn ☎ 01492 660504

Also in the series:

Llŷn Cycle Guide

by Phil Horsley

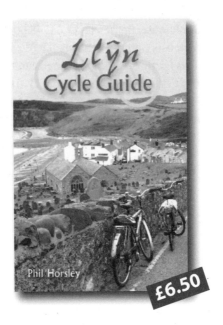

This comprehensive guide offers clear, informative cycle routes for everyone from family to the experienced cyclist, and tells you all you need to know about the culture and life of the people of Llŷn.

Also in the series:

Anglesey Cycle Guide

by Phil Horsley

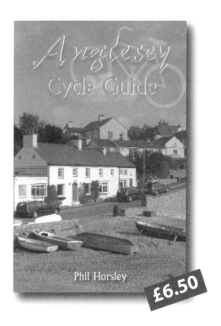

£6.50

This comprehensive guide offers clear, informative cycle routes for everyone from family to the experienced cyclist, and tells you all you need to know about the culture and life of the people of Anglesey.

Further enjoyable reading on History and Heritage

Visit our website for further information:
www.carreg-gwalch.com

Orders can be placed on our
On-line Shop